10,000 Days:

The Rest of Your Life, the Best of Your Life

To Dion —
You are such a beautiful person — your energy & COURAGE inspire me ! Here's to your next 10,000 Days ! All my best.
T. Hinton Hinton
3-29-2013

Tom Hinton

www.10000DaysFoundation.org

tom@10000DaysFoundation.org

ISBN: 978-0-9835032-1-7

Tom Hinton

Author & Speaker

tom@tomhinton.com

Blue Carriage
Publishing Company

Post Office Box 503016
San Diego, CA 92150-3016
info@bluecarriage.com

Disclaimer

The purpose of this ebook is to educate and empower. The author does not guarantee that anyone following these ideas will have specific results. The author shall have neither liability nor responsibility to anyone with respect to any loss or damage caused, or alleged to be caused, directly or indirectly by the information contained in this ebook. This work includes both factual occurrences and fictitious representations including certain names of individuals and places. The author also uses anecdotes, conversations and fictional representations to convey the story of *The Course of 10,000 Days*®.

ACKNOWLEDGMENTS

As every author knows, a book is rarely the work of one person. It takes many people to spark an idea, synthesize concepts and mold that idea into a successful product. I am grateful to many people who have contributed to the writing, production and publication of *10,000 Days: The Rest of Your Life, the Best of Your Life.*

Dr. Leif Livingheart, my spiritual advisor and a gifted thought leader; Eileen Murray-Giles, who always took time away from life in London and Sydney to help me stay focused; Jared Kuritz of PR Strategies in San Diego, who has guided this project to fruition; Jody Sims, a great graphic designer and innovative cover designer; Signe Nichols and Aaron Ciampi, of Firebird Web Design, who shaped the www.10000Days.org website; Andrea Glass, of the Writers Way, who edited the early manuscripts; my dear, late friend, Gary Plantz, who contributed so much encouragement, wisdom and support over the past 35 years; my friend, the late Brian Klemmer, of Klemmer & Associates, who always had positive thoughts and suggestions along this journey; and, Malcolm Franks, who challenged me "not to write rot or it will never sell!"

I am also very grateful to my *10,000 Days* Planning Day Team, who refined *The Course of 10,000 Days* Weekend Retreats and delivered invaluable support to this project. They include: Mark Rosenberger, CSP; Chris Knudsen; Sheryl Roush, Speaker and Author; Suzan Tusson, speaker and author of Women at P.L.A.Y; Marianne Pinto; Dr. Holly Hunt, speaker and author of Emotional Exorcism; Claudio Stemberger, Thought Leader, Author and Philosopher; Karla Olson of Book Studio and the person who helped me create the sub-title for this book; Lori Sheets, spiritual counselor; John Mutz, Executive Coach in Santa Rosa, California; Scott Hunter, author and speaker; Kane Phelps, speaker and author; Jeff Salz, Ph.D., speaker and author; Lisa Jaffe, seminar leader; Bob Ross, the Corporate Comic; Carolyn Gross, R.N., speaker, author and seminar leader; Joni Wilson, my talented voice coach and producer of the audio version of 10,000 Days. Finally, I am most grateful to my wife, Jean, and my daughters, Megan and Rebecca, for whom this book is dedicated because love and legacy ultimately are what matter most in life and it's all we really leave behind.

Tom Hinton
San Diego, CA
September 20, 2012
tom@10000days.org

Contents

Part Three — Acceptance of the Divine

Part Four — Embracing the Power of Love

PART ONE

Acceptance
of Self

CHAPTER ONE

The Laguna Beach Conversation

There are moments in life when a nurturing, internal force challenges us to overcome our limitations and achieve our dreams. The nurturing force I am referring to is our Inner Spirit. Its power is so profound that you can change your thoughts, behaviors, actions and outcomes. I know this to be true because it is the very transformation I made as a result of experiencing *The Course of 10,000 Days®*.

Oftentimes, our Inner Spirit surfaces when we are most vulnerable—when we are struggling with changes in our life, when a relationship is broken or failing, when we are in financial trouble or workplace pressures seem overwhelming. It's during these difficult and trying times that our Inner Spirit—that conscious, spiritual dimension of our Being that balances our ego and emotions—surfaces to gently nudge us towards our higher purpose and help us achieve success and happiness.

When your Inner Spirit emerges, it is ready to help you answer such unsettling questions as *Who am I?* and *How do I give my life meaning and purpose?* Like a blade of grass inching its way above the soil in search of sunlight and the earth's nutrients, your Inner Spirit quietly persists until you acknowledge its presence. Only then can our Inner Spirit unleash its powers.

It was during such a moment that I was introduced to *The Course of 10,000 Days®*. Although it occurred several years ago, I remember it as if it happened yesterday. I was having dinner at Las Brisas restaurant in Laguna Beach with my client and friend, Ajay Shivani. Ajay and I met several years ago when I was retained by his company, which I refer to in this book as The Global Corporation (TGC), to serve as his leadership coach. Our professional relationship lasted two years. During that time we became friends and would often visit socially or play golf whenever our schedules permitted.

Ajay was born in India in the Chowpatty section of Mumbai not far from the Hanging Gardens perched at the top of Malabar Hill. His work values and standards were shaped during high school while working part-time for the Indian Railways where his father had a management position overseeing the regional Freight Operations Information System. At a young age, Ajay developed an interest and appreciation for science and technology by watching his father modernize the complex freight operation system for India's railway. His father also taught Ajay to respect people and treat them with dignity regardless of their job title, religion or social status. Ajay attended Oxford University and after completing his Masters Degree program, he accepted a management position with TGC in California.

As we dined together at table 17 at Las Brisas, I shared with Ajay the frustration, stress and aggravation of managing my growing business and balancing my life priorities. He listened quietly to my woes and then told me an intriguing story about how his life had been transformed by a philosophy he learned a few years earlier from a boyhood friend, Dr. Kavi Chavan. Dr. Kavi, as Ajay referred to him, was a respected cardiologist at Breach Candy Hospital in Mumbai.

Ajay referred to his transformational experience as *The Course of 10,000 Days*®, or simply, *The Course*. Ajay said *The Course* changed his life by helping him learn how to control his ego, balance his emotions and reconnect with his Inner Spirit. In the process, Ajay discovered his higher purpose and achieved many of his life goals and dreams. He challenged me to complete *The Course*.

At first I was reluctant. I pictured in my mind a motivational seminar demanding I perform extreme exercises like walking across a fiery bed of hot coals or standing up in front of strangers to bare my soul. Over the past 25 years, I had attended my share of corporate meetings and rah-rah rallies, and listened to hundreds of motivational speakers who made me feel good for a few hours but didn't have the ability, know-how or power to truly transform lives. So, yes, I was reluctant. However, I gave the decision serious thought as we enjoyed the spectacular view of the Pacific Ocean at table 17, ate our enchiladas and drank a Hess Chardonnay wine.

I challenged Ajay on several points about *The Course* including his premise about a higher purpose and the ability of our Inner Spirit to shape our destiny and outcomes in life. Ajay listened patiently to my arguments and then replied, "If you have a better answer, you should pursue it. But if you are like the majority of people who are living lives of quiet desperation, as Thoreau wrote, I would encourage you to explore *The Course* and create new possibilities for yourself."

I asked Ajay what happens if the clock runs out before we discover our higher purpose and achieve our destiny. Ajay reflected for a moment then told me, "Well, Tom, it's a bit like Beethoven's 10th Symphony, which the great composer never finished. It remains a work-in-progress for others to complete. *The Course* tells us that our unfinished journey on earth will fall to someone else.

"Our human death is not finality. It's akin to hitting the reset button for life. All the great spiritual teachers remind us that human life is only one phase of our existence. This is why everything matters—nothing is inconsequential. Regardless of our past achievements, failures, limitations or dreams, if we begin now to create a life worth remembering—and allow our Inner Spirit to surface and guide us—there's a good chance we will discover our higher purpose and find passion and peace in our life. This is what *The Course* can offer you. It is but one proven path to happiness and fulfillment."

There was no hard sell or arm twisting on Ajay's part to enroll me in *The Course of 10,000 Days*®. While Ajay encouraged me to pursue it, he left the decision completely in my hands. Before leaving Las Brisas that evening, I agreed to undertake *The Course*.

This book is about my journey and struggles to complete *The Course*. It was certainly one of the most difficult challenges I have ever undertaken because it forced me to confront the real me and change what needed to be changed if I ever wanted to achieve more goals and dreams.

By following my journey, I hope you will embrace the principles and teachings of *The Course,* and come to recognize your unlimited potential and higher purpose. If so, perhaps, you will want to enroll in *The Course of 10,000 Days Weekend Retreat*® and take the next step to change your life so that you too can achieve your unfulfilled goals and dreams, and discover your higher purpose.

CHAPTER TWO

30,000 Days

In introducing me to *The Course*, Ajay told me the average person lives about 30,000 days. He referred to a person's first 10,000 days, which equates to a little more than 27 years, as their *Discovery Years*. These days span our infancy to early adulthood. We spend our Discovery Years developing our personality and ego, learning values, shaping our character and behavior and creating lifelong bonds with our family and friends. It is during our Discovery Years that we attempt to discover our gifts and talents and exercise our creativity. We also learn how to assess risks, make mistakes and rebound, expand our minds, learn social graces, receive a formal education, plot our career path, forge our political beliefs and values, challenge the status quo, set goals and discover the power and pitfalls of money and romance.

Our second 10,000 days are our *Fulfillment Years*. Most people spend their Fulfillment Years building their resume, acquiring wealth, searching for and finding true love, starting a family, laying down roots, striving to achieve their goals, traveling and consuming all the world has to offer.

Ironically, as many people complete their Fulfillment Years they realize they are, in fact, *unfulfilled* because they have failed to live their dreams or achieve their vision and goals. They notice that their Fulfillment Years have been reduced to climbing the corporate ladder, chasing success and keeping up with the Joneses. It's a stark moment in our lives when we come to the realization that we are completely ego-driven and have little connection with our Inner Spirit, nor any reasonable explanation as to why we exist.

When we arrive at this awkward point in our life, it marks the beginning of a major transformation in our life. It is the point when we come face-to-face with our third 10,000 days, which *The Course* refers to as our *Legacy Years*. It is at this moment we grasp that something significant in our life is missing. As weeks and months pass, the internal rumbling within our gut and deepest emotions get louder. This is not our ego at work but something much stronger and positive that appears to know the answers to such nagging questions as *Who am I? How do I live a life worth remembering?* and *What is my higher purpose in life?* It is the gentle, steady voice of our Inner Spirit.

When we reach this turning point in our lives, we begin to ask our Inner Spirit to help us find meaningful answers to these difficult questions that will shape our next 10,000 days. It is hard to get on with our lives until we have some rational explanation as to why we exist and what our higher purpose is on earth. It's typical for people in their mid-40s and early 50s to start asking themselves such somber questions about life's meaning and purpose as they experience the death of loved ones—parents, a spouse, family members and friends. With each personal loss, the pressure to satisfactorily answer these unsettling questions intensifies and we hunger for meaningful answers. When loved ones pass away, a serious void is created in our life and we realize our ego is incapable of answering these humbling questions.

This spiritual void is one reason why so many people enter their third 10,000 days—our *Legacy Years*—anxious, unfulfilled and searching for answers. This is why so many 40 and 50-year olds undergo a mid-life crisis and walk away from their careers, marriages and families in search of something new. We also neglect our health and other essential elements associated with the Wheel of Life (see page 256). But without clarity of direction, conviction of purpose and confidence in one's self, these wandering souls are doomed to a life of ambiguity and unanswered questions.

During our Legacy Years, we struggle with two fundamental issues. The first deals with human vanity. We begin to show our age in unflattering ways. We also begin to show signs of mortality. Our body doesn't work as well as it used to and we start sagging in certain places and expanding in others. We would rather ride in a golf cart than walk the links. Our bones begin to ache and given the choice, on a cold December morning, we would rather stay in a warm bed than face the frost to walk the dog or exercise our creaking bones. We require reading glasses to see the small print in the morning paper or decipher our emails on the computer monitor. We forget the names of people we just met yesterday. It's very disconcerting for most of us. This is why so many people in their 40s and 50s join fitness clubs and undergo plastic surgery. While I have not resorted to plastic surgery, I did join a fitness club to lose the 30 pounds I had accumulated since graduating from college and being married to a brilliant cook!

The second issue relates to our personal legacy and how we will be remembered. This was the primary focus of our Laguna Beach conversation. Ajay and I talked at length about the importance of creating meaning and purpose in our lives so we could feel a sense of accomplishment.

As we concluded our dinner conversation, Ajay offered to teach me *The Course of 10,000 Days*®. He also challenged me with some assignments— some field work to help me achieve meaningful answers and results during *The Course*. I told him I would do it as long as he would be my teacher.

"I am merely the witness," Ajay replied. "You must be your own teacher. As the Buddhist monk Ajahn Chan said, 'Looking for teachers will not solve your doubts. You must investigate yourself to find the truth. It is hidden on the inside, not the outside. Knowing yourself is most important.'"

CHAPTER THREE

The Three Sacred Questions

Before concluding our dinner at Las Brisas, Ajay told me about The Three Sacred Questions. He said these questions were the heart of *The Course* and everything I learned would revolve around my ability to answer them candidly. It was then that Ajay revealed the first of the Three Sacred Questions of *The Course*: *How do I celebrate the gift of life?* He also told me that each Sacred Question has three tenets which I would need to answer. The three tenets of the First Sacred Question are:

What are my gifts that make my life unique and special?

How do I share my gifts with others?

How do I use my gifts to create a better life for myself and others?

As we left Las Brisas and walked through its beautiful rose garden that overlooked the magnificent Pacific Ocean below, Ajay told me the red rose is the symbol of *The Course*. It represents the power of rebirth and transformation. He said, "If you have ever grown roses then you know they need to be nurtured in order to bloom. And once the flowers have bloomed, a rose bush needs to be pruned back so it can rejuvenate itself. *The Course of 10,000 Days*® requires the same of us. It requires us to be a gardener of sorts. We must plant a seed that we nurture and then oversee our own growth and development. And so, you are the rose and I am your gardener." The rose, as I learned, also symbolizes The Kingdom of Roses, which I discuss in Chapter 25.

Over the next three months, Ajay guided me through *The Course*. We had several conversations while attending business conferences in Lake Tahoe, Vancouver, Dublin and Baltimore. What I learned from Ajay and others on my journey is shared with you in this book.

The goal of *The Course* is to help you discover and live your higher purpose. Everything you will read and learn in this book flows from this goal.

The Course consists of four parts:

Acceptance of Self. During the first part, you will examine your life by answering The Three Sacred Questions. Through this introspective process, you will decide what you want to achieve during your next 10,000 days. Allow yourself to dream big. There are no limits.

Acceptance of Others. In part two, you will explore The Three Sacred Questions in greater depth and cross over the *Bridge of Forgiveness* by forgiving those who have offended you and seeking forgiveness from those you have offended.

Acceptance of the Divine. This part prepares you to enter *The Kingdom of Roses* by overturning the Four Stones that prevent your access to this spiritual state of grace where the inherent powers of the Divine Source and your higher purpose are revealed to you. The Four Stones are the four imperfections of the ego that we must overcome in order to reconnect with our Inner Spirit and find purpose, peace and passion in our life.

Embracing the Gift of Love. It is during this final part that you celebrate your higher purpose by embracing your infinite powers and living the greatest of those powers, the gift of love, through your words and deeds. This is how you will attain grace, peace and happiness in your life.

I wrote this book to help those of us who are entering our Legacy Years and are yearning for meaningful answers to life's most difficult questions including: *What is my higher purpose in life?* and *How do I live a life worth remembering?* Answering these two questions represent a turning point in a person's life. Interestingly, that turning point is not defined by age, but rather by opening our hearts to new possibilities—a state of readiness, if you will. Whenever our Inner Spirit senses we are receptive to its overtures, it surfaces and invites us to respond to its call. Sometimes, this invitation comes to us disguised as stress, doubt, problems, uncertainty or fear. The reason for the disguise is to get our attention. Very few people hear the call of their Inner Spirit when things are going well and their ego is in control.

Some people who are lost or drifting aimlessly through life falsely believe there is something wrong with them—emotionally or spiritually—because they lack a relationship with God or they sense their life is on the wrong track. I can tell you that with very few exceptions these are merely hurdles and challenges everyone faces. Obviously, there is a major difference between mental imbalance and having a void in our life. *The Course* teaches us that the sooner we can satisfactorily answer those haunting questions that continue to nag us, the sooner we will find our purpose, experience peace and discover our passion in life. This is why each of our 10,000 days is precious. As I learned from Dr. Kavi and *The Course*: "All my somedays are today!"

I have also written this book for those who are awakening from a period of spiritual deprivation and want to re-connect with their Inner Spirit. Perhaps, you are like me and yearn to make the journey to that special place that lies deep within you where life is more satisfying and rewarding. I can tell you—having made the journey—it is a place everyone can reach. But I must also tell you it requires a personal commitment to become the person you dream about. It requires focus, persistence and diligence to get there.

That evening in August as I left Las Brisas and wound my way down the Pacific Coast Highway through Laguna Beach towards Interstate 5, the sidewalks and shops were bustling with tourists and artists who were attending the Laguna Beach Arts Festival. The Friday evening traffic had thinned somewhat but there was still a steady stream of cars ahead of me. The congestion gave me time to reflect on what Ajay had told me, especially with regards to our unlimited potential and making the most of our time on earth.

CHAPTER FOUR

Balancing Your Ego,
Emotions and Inner Spirit

*T*he Course of 10,000 Days® is based on a simple life-balance
philosophy that encourages your ego and Inner Spirit to work
together in harmony so you can live your dreams and attain your
higher purpose. While *The Course* is not aligned with any single religion
or philosophy, it complements the wisdom from the greatest teachers,
saints and philosophers throughout the ages.

On your journey, you will repeatedly meet yourself; and, every
encounter will afford you a new opportunity for self-examination, truth,
awareness, forgiveness, acceptance, growth and inner peace. Each
encounter will bring you closer to your ultimate spiritual destination, a
state of mind *The Course* refers to as The Kingdom of Roses. It is in The
Kingdom of Roses that you will discover your higher purpose and the
secret to a life worth living. It is in The Kingdom of Roses that you will
find that level of internal peace you have sought all these years. Having
said this, *The Course* will test you intellectually and spiritually because it
demands that you balance the four aspects of your total self—Being,

Thinking, Feeling and Doing—before you can enter The Kingdom of Roses.

As you embark on *The Course of 10,000 Days*®, you will be asked to examine your life very closely and truthfully. Each question, exercise and phase of *The Course* has been carefully developed and refined over many years. If you have self-doubts, as I did, remind yourself that this phase of your life is a journey of 10,000 days. As Ajay Shivani told me, "I spent 50 years allowing my ego and emotions to control my life. I decided to spend a few days mastering *The Course* to learn how to reconnect with my Inner Spirit so I could finally give meaning and purpose to the rest of my life."

For some, the answers will appear quickly, for others, it might take longer. Don't get frustrated. Be patient. Allow your Inner Spirit to surface and guide you through this transformational process.

Now that I teach *The Course*, I also try to improve myself and live up to the commitments I made as a student of *The Course*. There are times when living *The Course* demands all my patience and then some. I can also tell you that despite my best intentions to be the person I truly want to become, on occasion I still fall short. Yet, I know in my heart I am a better person today than I was yesterday. Also, I am much closer to achieving my life goals because I am living my higher purpose every day and allowing my Inner Spirit to surface more often and guide me to that Universal Truth most of us seek—acceptance of self and existing in a state of inner peace and love.

I understand there are people who struggle with serious illnesses, personal and family problems and dogged demons in their life. But I have learned the solutions are the same regardless of the obstacles we face. It is a matter of our intentions that makes the difference. In other words, what is it you desire from life? Whatever predicament you are faced with there is a solution. There is no valid reason to remain captive to the demons that torment you. This is true for people who suffer from drug and alcohol abuse, obesity, family feuds, lack of money, problems in the workplace and many illnesses. Change is not only possible through the power of your Inner Spirit, it is absolutely vital to achieving your dreams and becoming the person you desire.

For me, this change represented a major mind-shift in becoming the person I wanted to be. Before, whenever I was confronted with an emotionally-charged decision, I allowed my first emotion to dictate my response. Usually, my response was negatively charged as I lashed out at the messenger. That only made matters worse. Now, I consciously choose to follow my Inner Spirit instead of my ego. I use the techniques I learned from *The Course* to control my temper, emotions and responses. Now, in my thoughts and actions, I consciously try to be more understanding, kind, respectful and fair with others.

In life, *like* attracts *like*. I want to attract success and happiness into my life. While I make mistakes every day, now I know my higher purpose and I strive to live it. I try to be more tolerant and forgiving of myself and others. I understand perfection is fleeting, but attaining a higher consciousness is very doable.

Perhaps, the most significant discovery I made during my study of *The Course* was recognizing the unlimited powers of my Inner Spirit. Since I experienced this breakthrough, I have been able to accomplish much more with less effort. You will be amazed at how much you can accomplish when your Inner Spirit is guiding you—instead of your ego and emotions. Doors will open for you and life will be infinitely improved! Throughout this book, I will share with you the secrets for unleashing the powers of your Inner Spirit and achieving your dreams and goals. As a matter of fact, I already have! Did you catch it?

Having said that, you should know there are inherent conflicts between your ego, emotions and Inner Spirit. Through *The Course*, I discovered how my ego had quietly seized control of my life and emotions in order to manipulate the decisions I made. It was recognizable in small ways.

For example, I found myself arguing and needing to be right which made other people wrong. I was judgmental and held grudges. I assessed blame and resented certain people who had wronged me. I also allowed my first emotion to dictate my response in confrontational situations. While I was not hostile, I was short-tempered and insensitive to others' feelings. Many times I acted selfishly and without love in my heart.

The Course helped me to understand why I acted this way and how to change it. Most people want to be happy in life. But *wanting* to be happy is tantamount to wishing and hoping. This is not where we should place our energy and efforts. *The Course* teaches us that true happiness is ultimately achieved by knowing our purpose in life, being at peace with ourselves and being passionate about our work and the people we associate with. To achieve this result, there must be a balance among our ego, emotions and Inner Spirit.

The Course refers to this balance as the *Triangle of Being*—that is, our Ego, Emotions and Inner Spirit. If you picture a triangle, you can visualize how each of the three dimensions of our Being support each other to create a manageable balance in our life.

Although each of these dimensions is equal, our ego often throws the *Triangle of Being* out of kilter by seizing control of our emotions and filling us with fear and false hope. The result is a lopsided and imbalanced state of mind that confuses us, paralyzes us from taking risks, making decisions and ultimately, plunging us into a state of unhappiness and despair because things do not turn out the way we want them to.

What happened? What went wrong? *The Course* explains it this way. The ego's agenda is to be in control so it can create certain outcomes and claim credit for our successes and achievements in life. However, the fact is no one can control life's outcomes. We can only chart a course, work our plan and have confidence that good things will happen as a result of our decisions and efforts. But our ego cannot accept this which is why it tries to manipulate our thoughts and emotions. It also tries to rationalize every inaction, bad decision or mistake we make in order to arouse our emotions in an effort to maintain control. The most devastating effect the ego has on the *Triangle of Being* is it justifies every negative situation in our life by attributing blame to somebody else. In other words, our inability to succeed in life or achieve our goals and dreams has nothing to do with us—the ego claims it's somebody else's fault! This is how the ego slyly remains in control. Ironically, our emotions play the role of a co-conspirator in all this drama by accepting the ego's warped logic and ill reasoning for why things go wrong.

While they are an equal part of the *Triangle of Being*, our emotions are easily manipulated and kept in check by the ego because we simply want to be happy. Also, our emotions sense the ego knows what it is doing because the ego is very loud and always has a plausible—albeit often flawed—explanation as to why things went awry.

The fact is our ego has no real answers; it only has questions. This is why the ego will frequently pose questions that begin with who, what, when, where and how? For example, if we are contemplating switching jobs, starting a new relationship or relocating to a different city, our ego will quickly pose questions that are fear-based in order to preserve the status quo and squash any changes. It doesn't matter if the changes we are considering are for the better because our ego does not like change.

This negative reflex on the part of our ego often creates roadblocks in our head and heart, and causes us to delay taking action even though we know instinctively that what we want to do is the *right* decision. *The Course* teaches us that self-doubt is the genesis of fear. It's the primary reason so many talented people never achieve their dreams and goals. It's the major reason so many people live a life of regret.

The ego tries to control our Being through three primary tactics—fear, hope and chaos. And because our emotions have been developed and nurtured through life experiences (both good and bad), we go along with the ego never questioning the consequences which are often disappointment, frustration and unhappiness. *The Course* taught me to ask an important question to calm my ego: *Would I rather be right or at peace?* You see, the ego always wants to be right even though it is often wrong. This question helps to quiet my ego and control my emotions and allows my Inner Spirit to surface and communicate with me.

It is in these desperate moments when we are disappointed with life or hit rock bottom that our Inner Spirit quietly surfaces to offer us a way out—an alternative direction. Unlike the ego, the Inner Spirit has no agenda. Its sole purpose is to guide us to our higher purpose in life. This is why our Inner Spirit speaks to us softly and with clarity, with no emotional attachment.

Nor does our Inner Spirit participate in all the theatrics or drama staged by our ego and emotions. Our Inner Spirit simply is. It knows better than to believe everything we think. It does not surrender to our emotions; it remains above the fray. What is most powerful about our Inner Spirit is that it understands instinctively the right path we should follow to achieve our higher purpose. In many respects, it is our trusty, reliable sixth sense and inner compass.

As Dr. Kavi noted, "Our Inner Spirit has a roadmap to success and happiness in life and beyond." It is through our Inner Spirit that we will discover our higher purpose, find lasting peace and experience a passion for living. Our Inner Spirit is, in fact, our Dao – that channel that leads us to the Christ within each of us.

Let me share with you an incident that helped me understand how my Inner Spirit was trying to surface so it could guide me and transform my thinking. I had been studying *The Course* for only three weeks when I traveled to Memphis for a speech. I checked into my hotel on a hot, humid September afternoon. I was tired from my long trip and ringing with sweat from the humidity and stifling heat that engulfed the Mississippi delta region that summer.

As I walked down the hotel corridor towards my guest room, I had to maneuver my luggage past a housekeeper's cart that was blocking the hallway. My first emotion was one of irritation because I couldn't get past the housekeeper's cart without pushing it aside. As I walked by an open guest room, I spotted an older Hispanic woman on her hands and knees scrubbing out the bathtub and cleaning the tile floor. It was *her* cart that was blocking the hallway. Suddenly, she turned towards the hallway and we made eye contact. She looked at me with her kind eyes and smiled. She said to me in her second language, English, "Hello, sir, can I help you?"

I quickly regained my composure and asked if she would be cleaning my guest room? She got up off her hands and knees and said, "Oh, yes sir. Do you have any special requests for me like extra towels or shampoo?" I was so touched by her personal commitment to service that I reached into my wallet and gave her $5. I said, "No, I just want you to know I appreciate all your hard work." She smiled and said, "Oh, bless you, sir. You are very kind. Thank you," and returned to the bathroom where she continued scrubbing the bathtub.

I walked a short distance down the corridor and went inside my hotel room. As I closed the door behind me, tears welled up in my eyes because I realized this woman, who made her living cleaning hotel guest rooms, had a more generous heart than me. Although I never said anything unkind to her, my intention was to reprimand her for something as trivial as blocking the corridor with her cart. It made me stop and ask myself,

"Is this how I treat others?" It made me realize I was the lesser person and in those moments when I allowed my ego to dictate my first emotion or put my selfish needs ahead of others, I was not living *The Course* or honoring my personal mission statement: to inspire, teach and nurture people in the ways of service, leadership and love. It was at that moment that my Inner Spirit surfaced once again and asked me a series of penetrating questions. I did not have any good answers except to admit that I was flawed, selfish and unhappy with who I was and how I treated others.

This was a defining moment for me and I made the conscious decision to change my thoughts, behaviors, actions and outcomes. Just as *The Course* had taught me, I resolved to give my very best to every person I met. I also resolved to find a positive, kind word to say to people and not talk down to or criticize them. No longer would I complain about the terrible trifles of life. As the song goes, I decided to accentuate the positive and see the 90% that people get right instead of the 10% that we botch! While this is difficult to do on a consistent basis, I am getting better at it with each passing day as I use the lessons and tools of *The Course*.

As a result of my encounter with that housekeeper in Memphis, and learning to connect with my Inner Spirit, I began to take small steps to consciously change my behavior and actions. I started with simple acts of kindness and forgiveness. For example, I stopped honking my car horn at other drivers and started to accept the many situations—both pleasant and unpleasant—that life on the highway hurls at me. I also started to let go and allow things to naturally unfold. This helped me get to a quieter place in my heart and mind where I no longer struggle to solve every problem. Instead, through my Inner Spirit, I learned how to stay present and find harmony with the moment.

In the process of allowing my thoughts and emotions to be controlled primarily by my ego, I was unknowingly suppressing my Inner Spirit. As

I became aware of this fact through *The Course*, I started to change my thoughts, control my emotions and create new and better outcomes in my life. I was elevated to a higher consciousness and this process helped me discover how to create a balance between my ego and Inner Spirit. It also helped me build lasting relationships, experience love, find peace and create happiness. I came to realize that these are the things that truly matter. Just about everything else in life is inconsequential. As the expression goes, too often we allow ourselves to major in the minors.

The Course also uses the teachings of Lao Zi and the symbolism of water to help students understand how to accept certain things and not allow our ego to meddle in the moment. During *The Course* retreat, we were instructed to place our index finger in a glass of water. We observed the water as it gently gave way. It did not resist. As we pulled our finger from the glass, the water quickly filled the void where our index finger had been. *The Course* reminds us that our Inner Spirit is like water. It will take on the shape of its container. Thus, if we allow certain events to unfold naturally, and without the intrusive ego, oftentimes issues will resolve themselves and turn out for the better.

Our Inner Spirit is like the water because it flows effortlessly and can adjust to changing environments. But if we punch our fist in the water, it erupts and splatters everywhere causing a mess. This is the effect the ego often creates when it injects itself into the fray. When our ego goes wild, accidents happen. Our lives are disrupted and we stray from our intended goals. Humanist philosopher and thought leader Claudio Stemberger reminds us that "the accidents of our lives often turn out to be the guiding forces by which we live." This is why so many people are guided by fear, desperation and a sense of hopelessness. They allow themselves to be controlled by their ego and not their Inner Spirit.

CHAPTER FIVE

We Are All Students
and Teachers

I learned from *The Course* that while we are all teachers, we are also all students. *The Course of 10,000 Days®* is a transformational experience because it requires you to spend time learning about yourself and reflecting on the life you want to live. *The Course* will ask you to open your mind and heart to exciting, new possibilities. It will introduce you to many of life's simple pleasures that you've ignored and it will ask you to let go of those things which you have no control over.

The Course will also challenge you to exorcise negative influences from your life which are toxic and keep you from living your higher purpose. This includes the *Old You* that labels you as the *Victim of Circumstances* and harbors grudges, anger and resentment towards yourself and others. It is through this transformational process, which is the foundation of *The Course*, you will change yourself and achieve your greatest goals and dreams. I tell you it is all possible because I have seen its power work, not only for me, but for many others. However, this process will require you to make some significant changes in how you choose to live your life—

the same changes Ajay and I were required to make.

I wish you peace and success on your journey to discovering your higher purpose and reconnecting with your Inner Spirit. I know *The Course of 10,000 Days*® will answer many of life's most challenging and difficult questions for you as it did for me. Most importantly, *The Course* will help you create the life you want, strengthen your relationships, aid you in achieving your goals and dreams and enrich the content of your life.

CHAPTER SIX

The Foundation of
The Course of 10,000 Days®

The concepts and teachings of *The Course of 10,000 Days*® are aligned closely with many of the most imperative philosophical, metaphysical and theological questions of our time. What mankind has struggled with for many millennia are philosophy, religion and science. We have also struggled to explain the existence of man, the world we live in and life itself. The platform of thought which great thinkers have used to explain these issues are unique and vary widely. One such group of learned men—Alberto Moravia, Umberto Eco and Alessandro Manzoni—presented their thoughts through prose in a soft, nurturing way. Others, including Immanuel Kant, Benedetto Croce and Plato presented their thoughts more pragmatically. Still, Thomas Aquinas, Martin Luther and Augustine of Hippo took another approach using religion and faith to support their beliefs and disseminate their theology.

Intelligent and reasonable people may disagree on the origins of the universe, the meaning of man and our purpose in life. Yet, all learned people acknowledge that anatomically, we're all part of the same universe. Biologically speaking, we're connected to all living things; and, chemically, we're connected to and dependent on our planet and universe. These conclusions do not require someone to understand science, or have great faith or embrace a particular philosophy. But, it does require us to understand and accept our relationship to all living things and, specifically, an understanding and acceptance of ourselves as human beings. The root of understanding ourselves begins with the *Triangle of Being*.

While *The Course* respects and acknowledges these different spheres of thinking and influence, it also serves as a bridge from what *is* to what is *possible*. Thus, regardless of one's faith, beliefs, values and philosophy we can find our truth, passion and higher purpose by re-discovering and cultivating our Inner Spirit. Our Inner Spirit is within us. It simply needs to be nurtured and developed.

The strength of *The Course* is that it acknowledges that each person has his/her own unique makeup—that is, our own values, beliefs, thoughts and personality. How we manifest our values, beliefs, thoughts and actions on a daily basis is what moves us towards our higher purpose— or hinders our progress. For example, each day we function with our own vocabulary. It is developed over a lifetime of experiences and is based on our beliefs, values and thoughts. It is also part of our uniqueness. But sometimes we lose consciousness and put ourselves on auto-pilot. The end result is we forget what we're thinking or saying. This type of random, irrational behavior allows our ego to usurp control of our emotions, thoughts and actions and, in turn, leads us down a perilous path.

Because we create the world we live in through our emotions, thoughts and deeds, we must not only be aware of them, but also we must change them from a negative influence in our life to a positive source of energy. This transformation paves the way for us to find our higher purpose and experience inner peace and passion. This is one way *The Course of 10,000 Days*® transforms people from a state of hopelessness and discontent to a state of pleasure, bliss and fulfillment.

Our greatest teachers have taught us that each human being is unique and special. Many of our greatest thinkers—from science, philosophy and religion—believe we were created in the image and likeness of a higher power. *The Course* not only accepts this premise but defines this higher power as the Divine Source. *The Course* teaches us that we entered this world as perfect beings and therefore, capable of attaining divineness— not in the metaphorical sense where we can change water into wine or rise from the dead, but rather in the sense that we can return to a state of perfect grace and complete love during this lifetime.

As the *Triangle of Being* suggests, we are born with an ego, emotions and an Inner Spirit. As infants we know only two things: survival requirements (such as crying, feeding and sleeping) and love. *The Course* refers to this condition as the *Impulse of Life*. And as we progress from infancy to adulthood, our ego develops rapidly and overshadows our Inner Spirit to the point where the Inner Spirit is almost forgotten and neglected.

Then, as subtly as it faded away, our Inner Spirit returns when we most need it—as we struggle through our Fulfillment Years trying to understand our true identity and unravel our higher purpose. Quietly, our Inner Spirit emerges and offers to guide us to our higher purpose and an enlightened existence. Through this cycle-of-discovery process many people change their life direction and emerge as renewed spirits capable of doing incredible things. Through this process we can attain our divineness on earth.

For this reason *The Course* believes that divineness is not only within each of us, but attainable. Jesus advocated this same principle in Mark's gospel (Chapter 9:23) when he said, "Through him all things are possible." The reference to our Inner Spirit is clear and undeniable. However, discovering our divineness and applying it to achieve our goals and dreams is an arduous process. It requires the coordinated effort of both our ego and Inner Spirit working in harmony with our emotions to help us overcome our human imperfections.

The Course of 10,000 Days® also aligns closely with universally accepted teachings and doctrines on the spiritual powers of human beings. Ajay reminded me that Eastern cultures and India's spiritual teachings, which have existed for thousands of years, embrace a similar theme as *The Course.* Those teachings and philosophies have been refined and tested over millennia. To this point, Ajay shared with me Will Durant's brilliant description of India:

India is the mother of us all; through Sanskrit, the mother of Europe's languages, through the Buddha, of the ideals embodied in Christianity, through the Arabs, of higher mathematics and algebra; through the village community, of self-government and democracy. Mother India is, in many ways, the mother of us all.

Regardless of one's culture, philosophy or religious beliefs, our greatest human quest remains the same: to give one's life meaning and purpose by discovering our divineness, since we have been made in the image and likeness of the Divine Source. These are the very issues all enlightened human beings seek to resolve regardless of their philosophical beliefs or religious roots. This is why *The Course* is consistent with the oldest teachings and beliefs in the world.

Finally, the basic teachings and principles of *The Course* come from many of the same inspirational teachings and doctrines you and I already understand and embrace. For example, if you subscribe to the concept that each of us has a higher purpose, and if you believe that your Inner Spirit lives beyond your physical lifetime as *The Course* advocates, then you also believe that every person has the potential to transcend their human form and experience divineness through their Inner Spirit.

The Vedas, the oldest sacred texts of Hinduism, tell us God is infinite and everywhere, around us and within us. In other words, we possess divine attributes because the Divine Source is within us perpetually. Thus, it makes sense that we should have the potential to enjoy fulfillment and happiness on earth with the tools the Divine Source has already given us.

The challenge we face is tapping into that potential. As Albert Einstein once quipped during a lecture at Princeton University, "Human beings only use about five percent of their brain power. Imagine what we could accomplish if we doubled that percentage!" Yet, despite the fact that each of us is unique and special, too many people "lead lives of quiet desperation and go to their grave with their song still in them," as Ajay reminded me when quoting the words of Henry David Thoreau. Others lead remarkable lives and accomplish great things. *Why is this?* Through *The Course,* the answer was revealed to me.

CHAPTER SEVEN

Finding Your Higher Purpose

At the root of *The Course* is the key question: *What is my higher purpose? The Course* teaches us that our higher purpose transcends the ego's needs and energizes our Inner Spirit to reveal our greatest attribute, which is love. *Knowing* the answer to this question is not much help at this stage of your journey because *knowing* is not the key to achieving your dreams and living a life worth remembering. The key to achieving your dreams is *living* your higher purpose. To do this you must make the journey and discover how to fill your life with love. By completing the journey, you discover your higher purpose and live a life worth remembering.

My greatest challenge in completing *The Course* was no different than most people's—learning how to quiet my ego so my Inner Spirit could surface. This was not an easy task because I was very ego driven. My Inner Spirit had been suppressed for decades by a strong ego and extroverted personality. It took a great deal of work and patience on my part to resurrect my Inner Spirit and bring it to the surface so I could connect with the Divine Source and find balance in my life.

Another part of the struggle you will face in transitioning from your Fulfillment Years to your Legacy Years is getting beyond the realm of the familiar, which is controlled by your ego, and moving to that unique spiritual place which is the domain of your Inner Spirit. Ironically, your ego will try to hold you back by telling your subconscious that you will have little control if you allow your Inner Spirit to surface. However, the truth is your *ego* will have little control.

This is why we must develop a different level of trust. For it is through our Inner Spirit that we discover the energy of our unconscious mind and learn how to transform that energy into our untapped divineness. This is the process *The Course* uses to help you attain your higher purpose and develop each person into a more powerful and enlightened being.

The *Bhagavad Gita*, one of the oldest and most respected Indian spiritual teachings, reminds us that there must be joy, peace and satisfaction in what we do in life. If those elements are missing then life becomes a burden and struggle. *The Course* complements these ancient spiritual teachings by helping us transition from the past to the present so joy, peace and satisfaction is possible.

Also, *The Course* teaches us that the only benefit of looking to the past is to learn from it. If you cannot learn from the past, it is meaningless to replay yesterday's decisions because you cannot change them. Life is about the present. While we should value the lessons learned from the past and cherish our memories, we cannot remain stuck in the "Velvet Rut"—that state of mind where we are too comfortable with the status quo to change our ways. We must push on. And as far as the future is concerned, it has not happened yet. The only place where we can make things happen and have some influence on the outcome of tomorrow's results is in the *Now*—at this very moment. Too many people are consumed with the regrets of yesterday or the fear and uncertainty of tomorrow.

Why is this? Because our ego tries to relive the past in order to rationalize certain decisions we made and make them right. When we allow our ego to rule our thoughts and control our emotions, we are out of balance. We are suppressing our Inner Spirit which is our link to the Divine Source and the only true path to discovering our higher purpose.

It isn't that our ego intentionally works against us. It is that our ego is programmed to perform two key functions: self-preservation and self-gratification. This is why our ego is always concerned with keeping the past alive and filling us with either fear, which holds us back or hope, which creates anticipation for the future. The ego is uncomfortable operating in the realm of the *here and now* because that is the domain of our Inner Spirit.

Through *The Course,* I began to understand what was missing in my life. My frustrations and agitations were due in large part to my inability to escape the stranglehold of my ego and allow my Inner Spirit to surface. I did not allow my total Being to function because of my ignorance and inability to understand that the mind is just one tool in our human toolbox. We can use it to reflect on the nostalgia and memories of the past, worry and fret about what might happen tomorrow or enjoy the here and now as we live and experience each moment to its fullest.

CHAPTER EIGHT

Defining Terms Used in
The Course of 10,000 Days®

As you study *The Course* it will be helpful to know the definition of certain terms. "Too often," Ajay reminded me, "when we learn things without context, it causes confusion and misrepresentation. It also allows critics to undermine the integrity of a principle or concept." This is why every term in *The Course* is defined. Here are some key definitions.

Science is defined by *The Course* as organized knowledge accumulated by continuous questioning and rigorous research with new and different conclusions drawn as evidence is presented. Science is the cumulative knowledge from multiple and diverse sources and principles that are universally accepted once they are proven by consistently producing the same results. Discovering what is true is Science.

Religion is defined by *The Course* as a set of beliefs pronounced by a deity and perpetuated by an established organization that gives answers and comfort to its believers. Religion is irrational in the sense that it cannot be proven or disputed because its beliefs are based on faith. *The Course* teaches us that irrationality is part of the human experience. Because of religion, believers do not need proof. Faith is not simply accepting claims for which you have no evidence. It's also about trusting the source and accepting God as the truth.

Happiness is defined by *The Course* as appreciation for what we have and who we are rather than wishing to be someone else or wanting something much more than what we already have. Happiness is achieved when we are comfortable in our own skin, at this very time and place.

Death is defined by *The Course* as the inevitable consequence of birth. Any expression of life will ultimately culminate in death. For all living things—organic and non-organic—life and death is a continuum. Each of us comes into being and goes out of being. We all live and die, and our Inner Spirits transition to a larger universe. In religious terms, we know this concept as life everlasting because our souls are eternal.

Depression is anger directed inward. Too often, the brunt of our self-criticism and discontent is the self. Depression is often triggered by a serious failure or setback. We become so angry and upset with ourselves that we redirect our hostility and negative emotions inward instead of at the situation or another person. We blame ourselves for life's failures. Perhaps, we lost our job, experienced a broken relationship, suffered a financial setback or just can't seem to catch a break and win.

Whatever the reason, depression often has its roots in a negative self-image or distortion of our ability to overcome the odds and succeed at something. And when we fail, our self-identification and ego can plummet. The more we had riding on a certain outcome or scenario, the harder we fall when things go awry. Such hostile emotions and negative feelings can lead us into a depressive state and we become the victim instead of the hero.

Culture is defined by *The Course* as a consequence of lifestyles repeated in time by a group of people geographically separated from each other. Environment is often responsible for creating cultural differences. Too often, foolish behavior is repeated in the name of culture, but it is merely tradition, not culture.

Travel is defined by *The Course* as both a physical and mental transition. The creative mind can travel to many different worlds—including the Cosmos—without the use of our legs. *The Course* also embraces Henry David Thoreau's concept of travel as clarity of direction, persistence and determination. Thoreau wrote, "If one advances confidently in the direction of his dreams, and endeavors to live the life which he has imagined, he will meet with success unexpected in common hours."

Inner Spirit is defined by *The Course* as that all-knowing, intuitive, elastic, spiritual dimension within each human being that is a composite of all our finest qualities which express themselves in various forms: intellectually, creatively, sexually, physically, athletically, emotionally and spiritually. It is this dimension that allows us to experience our human divineness.

CHAPTER NINE

Creating a Basis for Truth

People approach life from their own unique perspective and position. Within each of us is a yearning to be authentic—to discover our truer selves and reach a higher level of consciousness where we can realize our hopes and dreams. This is not wishful thinking. It is a proven process that all great mystics experienced. This is why completing the transformation from an ego-driven mindset to one of a spiritually-guided being is so difficult. It requires us to undergo a radical change—quieting the ego and allowing our Inner Spirit to surface and be dominant.

Once our Inner Spirit resurfaces and begins to influence our thinking and actions, it will not allow us to live a *lie*. The lie *The Course* speaks of is often described as a life of deceit where we drift from day to day on auto-pilot and surrender control of our thoughts and emotions to our ego. Instead, as we allow our Inner Spirit to be heard, it helps us self-actualize and awaken our potential. This includes acknowledging and acting on our gifts and talents, which we will discuss later.

According to Abraham Maslow's Hierarchy of Needs, which dates back to 1943, we exist at different levels on a scale of needs. Maslow identified five levels: physiological, safety, love/belonging, self-esteem and self-actualization. For some people, life is about trying to earn a paycheck or pay the rent. For others, life is about enjoying the fruits of their success. Now, as a society, our goal is to raise people up so they can self-actualize and achieve their full potential. This is a moral responsibility that an enlightened society has to its citizens. This is also why *The Course* focuses on helping people define their beliefs and values and increasing their understanding of self. It is by knowing one's self that enlightenment and wisdom are possible.

Through its four phases, *The Course* helps people develop their potential and achieve their life goals. This is how *The Course* advances society—by guiding each person to their higher purpose—one person at a time. This is why *The Course* places a high emphasis on the Wheel of Life and its eight critical elements.

Frankly, it is easier said than done because there is so much negativity in the world. Yet, as I teach *The Course*, I am gratified to see more people rejecting the negative tactics of fear, hate, scarcity and war that have become the primary tools of extremists and dictators whose only motives are power and money. Through *The Course*, I have met thousands of people who are yearning for more substantive answers and solutions to their personal problems and the global challenges facing us. The world is restless and we yearn for meaningful answers. Enlightened individuals understand there is a need for both institutional solutions and insightful solutions.

When it comes to global issues and politics, we rely on institutional solutions. However, when it comes to personal problems and creating a life worth living, we need meaningful answers that rise from the depths of our soul. This is why millions of people around the world have joined together in community circles and thought groups to seek answers to life's daunting questions. This is why so many people have turned to meditation, learning forums and self-actualization programs like *The Course* for answers.

Also, people are growing impatient with the status quo that perpetuates greed and corruption and allows poverty, sickness, hunger and war to exist in our modern age. These are symptoms of a sick society and egotistical leaders who are trapped in the past and cannot envision a world built on the prosperity of many let alone helping people discover the path to purpose, peace and passion. This explains why millions of people from Egypt to China have risen up to challenge dictatorial regimes that suppress the basic human rights and freedoms of citizens.

What *The Course* clarified for me is that happiness, peace and love have little to do with one's religious affiliation or political allegiance. While the majority of churches and religions bring joy, peace and satisfaction to their followers, regrettably some religious and political institutions attempt to undermine human progress by issuing restrictive policies, rules and edicts in order to control the masses and promote their own selfish, ego-driven agendas.

Many of these organizations have suppressed basic human freedoms including happiness and speech by issuing ridiculous decrees such as infallibility, requiring women to forego an education and wear traditional garb covering them from head to toe; not allowing women to be ministers or priests and not allowing women to drive automobiles. Such practices have nothing to do with God or theology. They are merely tools used by ego-driven men to suppress people by disempowering segments of society and exerting authority over their believers and followers. It is simply a case of religious fanaticism taken to the extreme!

Fortunately, in this era of self-actualization and New Thought, people are questioning the status quo and challenging man-made rules that limit their thinking and attempt to inhibit their potential. *The Course* encourages people to chart their own spiritual path and think beyond the boundaries of self-imposed limitations while ignoring the institutional babble that inhibits spiritual growth and discredits our efforts to experience divineness on earth.

Happiness, love and spiritual fulfillment are values we acquire as we discover our higher purpose and live it. The reason so many traditional religions are not meeting the needs of people is they have become sidetracked with superfluous issues and political agendas that impede the spiritual development of their members. This also explains why so many traditional religions have lost their spiritual compass and are losing members. Studies show that a growing number of people are seeking alternative forums because they are frustrated with organized religion, not because they doubt its core beliefs, but because of the contradictions expressed between its teachings and actions. This has happened despite the fact that most of the world's great religions can trace their origins to one individual whose overwhelming mystical experience resulted in the formation of today's contemporary church or religious practice.

For example, Jesus taught us to love all people, especially our enemies and those who are less fortunate. But, there are some Christian leaders who openly advocate war—the most vulgar of all human deeds. Some Judeo-Christian and Islamic extremists and hypocrites are quick to condemn someone based on his/her race, color, ethnicity or sexual preferences forgetting that these people are also God's children. As Dr. Kavi says, "If Jesus can accept them, why can't his followers?"

The Course was created to help you find purpose, peace and passion in your life by allowing you to see into the deepest recesses of your heart and mind. You must know yourself honestly and openly before you can achieve greatness and fulfillment in life. As Socrates said, "An unexamined life is not worth living." *The Course* helps you examine your life through a series of questions and exercises designed to raise your consciousness and elevate your Inner Spirit. It is through your Inner Spirit that you ultimately discover who you really are and what your higher purpose is.

One of the most meaningful prayers I learned from *The Course* comes from Philippians 4:8. It goes:

Whatever is true,
whatever is noble,
whatever is right,
whatever is pure,
whatever is lovely,
whatever is admirable —
if anything is excellent or praiseworthy —
think about such things.

So much of what we think about and talk about is small-minded and limiting. Just look at the television programs we watch every night. Yes, they're entertaining, but they do little to enrich our spirit or heart. Much of what we absorb in terms of messages from government, the media and subject matter experts diminishes our thinking. This is because we blindly accept what is said by others instead of questioning it and thinking things through for ourselves. We also allow our ego to control and manipulate our untamed emotions, thoughts and responses to situations because it is easier to surrender than to combat fear and experience the discontent of pain when we doubt or challenge those in positions of authority.

When teaching *The Course*, I often find that the ego is the culprit in cases where people fall short of their goals or find themselves wallowing in despair, resentment and self-pity. Here is how *The Course* defines *Ego*. At the time of your birth, you came into this world as a perfect being. Yet, with each passing day, you acquired more life experiences and your unique identity was formed. You became a more complete personality. Your ego was shaped in this way. Everything you do, see, feel, hear, touch, sense or smell is processed by your ego and becomes part of your life experience and belief system. It also becomes part of your reality. Every day, your ego sees a world of good and bad, love and hatred, happiness and sadness and all the other dualities that exist in life.

Your ego internalizes all of these emotions and life experiences and this is how you become who you are—a human being full of unique ideas and experiences. At the same time, you are also a person who formulates judgments, biases, prejudices, beliefs and convictions. And while your ego is neither positive nor negative, it is cautious. As I mentioned in Chapter 7, the ego seeks to protect you from the negative forces of the world by controlling your thoughts through two dominant emotions: fear and hope. The ego injects fear in our minds based on negative experiences. And the ego can also instill hope in our minds when it wants us to focus on the positive side of life. However, when we identify too much with the future and come to rely on "our tomorrows," as *The Course* reminds us, we find ourselves in a tug-of-war between anxiety and fear. This is neither emotionally healthy nor helpful to living in the moment.

In many situations and circumstances, your ego is a good thing. But, because your ego has filed away all of your life experiences, it tries to control your life by keeping your mind in the past or the future. In many ways, your ego acts like a malfunctioning traffic light that is always stuck on yellow. If you only see the yellow caution light, you are unlikely to accelerate to a higher level of achievement. This is the mind game our ego plays with us. The ego fears loss of control, and because of this insecurity, the ego tries to keep us living in the past or hoping for the future. As a result, when our Inner Spirit is suppressed, we do not live in the present moment which, ironically, is where our future is shaped and our past is forgiven.

During *The Course* retreats, I frequently observe people struggling with the concept of their Inner Spirit to the point where they will dispute or deny its very existence. But the proof is in our Being. Every dimension of life and nature has balance. The Inner Spirit is what balances the ego. In terms of accepting the premise of the Divine Source, that is a matter of both experience and science. It should not be left solely to a matter of faith. Consider this point: do you think that a single human cell which measures less than a thousandth of an inch in diameter could conceive such a grand master plan as our universe and all living things? No. The evidence for a higher power is too overwhelming. There is insufficient capability within a single human cell, which is how mankind began and evolved. If this is the case, there must be a greater power or universal force at work in our universe. That universal force is the Divine Source.

The Course reminds us that truth lies in the understanding of opposites. If you look closely at the world, there is a positive-negative balance for everything and everyone. There is day and night, male and female, up and down, life and death, fire and rain, sunrises and sunsets, evil and good, happy and sad—the list goes on and on. It only makes sense that there is a higher intelligence and energy at work, which *The Course* refers to as the Divine Source. And if there is a Divine Source, our existence must be the result of the same power and energy that created all of life. Thus, it follows that people also possess a degree of divineness.

But because we think of ourselves in *human* terms, we do not see ourselves as divine nor as having divine powers. This is simply a case of ignorance. In other words, we cannot access our divine powers because we do not know what we don't know. As such, we are not in balance with our total Being. If we were in balance, we would certainly be using more of our brain power and natural intelligence as Albert Einstein suggested. The problem is our ego holds us back because it is unwilling to share control with our Inner Spirit to the point it cannot endorse or embrace our divineness. For our ego to do so would be an admission of its fragile co-dependence on the Inner Spirit.

Human beings are engineered this way. We, too, have a positive-negative balance—our ego and our Inner Spirit. This is not to imply that our ego is a negative force in our life, but rather, it confirms the genius of our spiritual and physical design.

CHAPTER TEN

Searching for Our Higher Purpose through Awareness

*T*he *Course* teaches us that every person has both a life purpose and a higher purpose. This, too, is part of the duality of our existence. Your life purpose is linked to your ego and your humanness—things like your career goals, family, finances, dreams and aspirations. It is your personal mission statement about the *what* and *where* of your life. In other words, *what* do you want to be professionally and *where* do you want to be financially and emotionally in life as you enter your Legacy Years? At the other end of the spectrum is your higher purpose which is linked to your spiritual essence and has to do with the *how*. And the only way you can discover the *how* and live your higher purpose is to connect with your Inner Spirit and live in the moment—to be here now. To achieve this you must establish balance with your total Being.

The challenge most people have—and very few people actually realize it—is they are out of balance with their Being. I am referring to the balance between our ego and Inner Spirit. This concept is one of the most difficult aspects of *The Course* for people to grasp because the ego is such a dominant force. Fortunately, the ego is uncomfortable in the present moment because it is unable to control our thoughts when we are thinking and living in the here and now. The *Now* is strictly the purview of our Inner Spirit. So, the ego tries to steer our mind to the future or trap us in the past to avoid dealing with the present moment. This is one reason why your ego constantly struggles with your Inner Spirit for control of your mind and thoughts.

It is through your Inner Spirit that you can reach an enlightened state that reveals your higher purpose. However, this is difficult to accomplish because we were raised to think of ourselves in terms of being *someone*. The concept of *Self*—who we see ourselves as—is very powerful. Our ego reinforces the Self thousands of times every day through our feelings, emotions, senses and constant self-gratification. We were not raised to cultivate our Inner Spirit, but rather to satisfy our ego's needs. This is why we constantly reinforce our ego by measuring our self-worth through socially-accepted standards such as our popularity in school, the number of friends we make, how many awards we win, whether or not we get invited to the school prom, the zip code where we live, which college we attend, whether or not we graduated from college, who we marry, whether or not we have children, how much money we earn, our rank or status at the time of our retirement and whether or not we drive a new car or an old clunker.

These are all ego indicators that are reinforced through television commercials, newspapers, social networking sites, magazine ads and conversations with family, friends and neighbors. It's also how most people judge us because they have also been programmed to measure themselves by these socio-ego standards.

Think about it for a moment. Isn't the measure of a person's worth much greater than the title on their business card? I'm sure most people would consider Mother Teresa or Gandhi to be great human beings who accomplished more in their lifetimes than the efforts of 10,000 people combined. But, they didn't carry a business card or have a fancy title. They did not concern themselves with the ego's trivial needs or desires.

If you judge people like Gandhi and Mother Teresa solely by the ego's standards, they didn't amount to much, did they? They acquired very few possessions and devoted their lives to helping people less fortunate than themselves. And they certainly lived on the wrong side of the tracks. So, we must be careful not to mistakenly judge people by such narrow and limited standards. The only way we can accurately assess people is by examining their whole Being—that is, both their ego and their Inner Spirit.

The Course teaches us to see the uniqueness in each person regardless of their social status. We cannot assume that one person is more worthy than another because that person's material wealth is greater. In the eyes of the Divine Source, we are all equal. This is what Jesus meant when he spoke about the burdens of the rich during his Sermon on the Mount. He said, "Blessed are the poor." He did not say, "Blessed are the rich" because Jesus understood the limited role wealth plays in discovering one's higher purpose.

At the same time, *The Course* does not condemn wealth, it affirms it. *The Course* suggests we renounce our old perceptions, not our possessions. *The Course* tells us that while we should enjoy our possessions, we must not covet them because all possessions are temporary—they only symbolize happiness, but they are not the true source of our happiness. Peace and contentment within are the ultimate sources of happiness. Those who rely too much on their material possessions lose their artificial happiness when they lose their possessions.

What *The Course* teaches us with regard to The First Sacred Question— *How do I celebrate the gift of life*— is *how* to find the path to celebrating purpose, peace and passion in our life by separating the ego's needs from our spiritual needs. This is a discovery process—one that leads us from a state of insecurity and fear to a higher level of existence whereby we are comfortable living in the moment and calming our mind through silence.

In the process of completing that separation and defining the differences between our ego and Inner Spirit, we learn that moving beyond the basic human requirements of self-preservation, survival and dealing with our fears pale in comparison to discovering the powers of our Inner Spirit. Among our Inner Spirit's greatest powers are the ability to exist in a state of grace, that is, a tranquil state of peace and love.

This is what the celebration of life is all about. To arrive at this place, we must discover our talents and put our gifts to good use. Making money is certainly a talent. But if we use our money to satisfy only our ego and not develop ourselves and improve the world around us, we will have squandered that particular talent in the eyes of the Divine Source. Using our talents to achieve financial success is a good thing because it not only allows us to help others in need, but when we are financially successful, we can invest in ourselves by reconnecting with our Inner Spirit to seek answers to the deeper questions about our higher purpose.

Consider the central question of how we celebrate the gift of life and its relationship to our state of happiness and peace. When you fight and argue with your spouse or children, at what point does your heart grow tired of this destructive style? It's only when you've reached that critical point in your thinking that your Inner Spirit is able to intercede and advise you to change your thoughts and behavior. In other words, the *internal you* must change.

Something inside must conclude that winning the argument is not as important as preserving and strengthening loving relationships. Something within you must tell you there is a better way to air your differences and opinions. Something inside you must tell you that when you allow fear to control your decisions, you will lose. When your ego demands that you must be *right*, you will not only lose the battle, but you will also alienate those you love because your actions and conceit polarize those who love you through your negative judgments, harsh opinions and emotional outbursts.

Your mind must dictate a new course of action so your behavior changes. This is how you consciously stop fighting and find a peaceful approach. This is also how you find happiness in life. Anyone who is at war with the world, or at war with themselves, will never find happiness until they first find forgiveness. Remember, that all wars—whether they are fought at home or across national borders—are the creation of fear and ego-driven people who substitute the insanity of anger, greed or fear for compassion and forgiveness.

This is also true on a global scale. At some point, the heart of a nation must tire of its violent ways and change its policies by changing its leadership. This is especially true of nations ruled by dictators. I do not know of a single instance where a civil society did not eventually overthrow its dictator because people eventually longed for a more peaceful, harmonious existence.

Ajay reminded me of the 14th Dalai Lama, Tenzin Gyatso's, response to the question, "How can you forgive the Chinese for invading Tibet and murdering so many of your fellow citizens?" The Dalai Lama simply replied, "It makes me feel better to forgive than to hate them."

Imagine the shock of Poland's communist regime in the 1980s when the labor union movement, Solidarity, rose up and went on strike in the shipyards at Gdansk. Their peaceful defiance inspired millions of people in Poland and around the world to rally to their cause for freedom; and, in the process, their actions paralyzed the communist regime in Poland. No dishonest regime can kill or imprison *all* its citizens.

At some point the regime must relent. This is why the repressive, dictatorial regimes of North Korea, Iran, China, Burma and other tyrannical governments will eventually collapse. They cannot suppress the freedom and Inner Spirit of their citizens forever. The advent of social networking has made it possible for citizens to mobilize and exert their influence. No repressive regime is safe in this age of higher consciousness and New Thought.

History has taught us that peaceful, non-violent efforts do succeed. It is pointless for governments to kill thousands of innocent people in order to achieve their devious desires. Besides, *peace cannot be achieved through war*. Jesus, Gandhi and Martin Luther King, Jr. showed us a better way by rejecting violence and enlisting the masses to bring about change through peaceful means.

What sustains hostility and war is fear. The ego fears losing control. This is why your ego doesn't want to surrender control of your mind and emotions to your Inner Spirit. The ego is perfectly content existing in the past and fantasizing about the future. This is the ego's way of keeping you in check. However, to answer the Three Sacred Questions honestly and thoroughly, you must allow your Inner Spirit to reveal itself, foster peace of mind and propose meaningful responses that lie deep within you. This also requires you to be in the Now. Otherwise, your responses will be compromised by the ego.

At the same time, *The Course* teaches us that your ego is *not* the enemy. The ego is only responding to years of conditioned behavior. It doesn't want to address the potentially unpleasant memories of the past by admitting you are less than perfect. This is why the ego rationalizes everything in favor of the Self. But, the truth is, we all have experienced moments of embarrassment and disappointment. We all have experienced despair and failure. It's part of life. The good news is we are not alone.

Most people, if honest with themselves, will acknowledge mistakes and disappointments in their past. It's part of our human frailty. But, the ego doesn't take comfort in knowing most of the world is screwed-up. Nor does our ego want to admit that our best friends, spouse and family members also have their dark secrets and suffered setbacks in their lives. It should not come as a surprise to anyone. It's simply part of life. It's the imperfection of our world. No one is perfect. We all have warts.

Fortunately, we can change the way we think and, in turn, behave. We can learn to replace violence with peace. We can learn to soften our judgments to neutral responses and give our Inner Spirit the opportunity to speak to us. These are the major transformations that *The Course* guides us through to help us discover our higher purpose. Interestingly, most of the self-administered analysis and healing we undergo in *The Course* is in the form of silence, reflection, calmness and candor. It is the process of allowing our Inner Spirit to guide us to a place where we are at peace with ourselves and not threatened by our ego or what others might think of us. It is a place where we simply come to accept ourselves for who we really are—warts and all—and not some imaginary character our ego would like us to be. This is the transformation we make when answering the Three Sacred Questions. It is a subtle, soothing and spiritual experience that calms our emotions, quiets our ego and allows us to experience a higher level of consciousness by elevating our thoughts and feelings through the Inner Spirit.

Some people think it takes a miracle to bring about such a transformation. But, I'm reminded of how Dr. Kavi defines a miracle. He says it's letting God do all the work. Fortunately, in completing *The Course,* the work is left to us.

Part Two

Acceptance
of Others

CHAPTER 11

The First Sacred Question:
How Do I Celebrate the Gift of Life?

Early morning is my favorite time for walking. It's peaceful and quiet just after sunrise. Dr. Ken Blanchard said, "It's important how you choose to enter your day. It's important to enter each day grounded in truth." Since hearing those words, I have tried to begin my day by walking, reading something positive and reciting my goals. I prefer a quiet environment with low light and a few moments to get my mind settled and start my blood flowing. Early morning is the time I choose to ponder peaceful thoughts, stimulate my brain with creative ideas and review my daily goals.

As I walked along the lush green fairways of Mt. Woodson golf course, I reflected on the First Sacred Question, *How do I celebrate the gift of life?*

I recalled something Ajay had told me. Most people don't search for the truth. Instead, they work just hard enough to do an adequate job, gain the knowledge necessary to advance in their career, make a decent living, raise their family and look forward to retirement. For most people, being smart is more important than being wise. As part of my commitment to *The Course*, Ajay encouraged me to strive for wisdom over knowledge. He told me, "There's more to life than just being able to answer Jeopardy questions!" I smiled wryly because Ajay knew I enjoyed watching that television program.

Ajay also told me that living a meaningful life requires the individual to become aware of whom he or she is. This is necessary to fully celebrate the gift of life and exploit our talents and gifts. Without addressing the phases of self-awareness, it is difficult to know who we are and what we are capable of achieving. This is what Socrates implied when he counseled us to "know thyself."

Ajay knew many people who were successful but admittedly, he knew very few people who had accomplished something *significant* in their lifetime. Ajay said, "Earning lots of money isn't too difficult. It requires a good idea, concentration, good timing, a degree of luck and the ability to make the right decision when the risks are low and the stakes are high. But, living a life of significance is more difficult because it requires us to dedicate ourselves to something much bigger than our ego-driven interests. It requires us to be willing to stand up for a cause that is just. In the process of defending that cause, we confront our biggest fears and learn to overcome them."

This is what makes for greatness—having the courage and fortitude to resist the temptation to succumb to the masses and, instead, fight on just as Jimmy Stewart did in the classic film, *Mr. Smith Goes to Washington.*

Ajay admired the trailblazers of history—Joan of Arc, Gandhi, Lincoln, Carnegie, Amelia Earhart, Churchill, Jane Addams, Einstein, Rutherford, Neil Armstrong and Buzz Aldrin, Dr. Martin Luther King, Jr., Nelson Mandela and Teddy Roosevelt—for their courage in the face of great adversity. These people achieved significance during their lifetime. And so do countless others whose simple acts of kindness make this a better world.

Joseph Campbell, the renowned author and expert on mythology, said, "I don't think there is anything as an ordinary mortal. Everybody has his own possibility of rapture in the experience of life. All he has to do is recognize it and get going with it."

The Course teaches that when we come into this world, we are given three inherent qualities—*Skill, Knowledge* and *Talent*. Skill and Knowledge are learned. But Talent is derived from the Divine Source. To live a life of significance, we must find a way to equally develop all three legs of our *Life Success Triangle* as it's referred to in *The Course*. I think about the Life Success Triangle whenever I recall the story of a gifted college athlete named Jim, who was seriously injured in a motorcycle accident.

Jim told his story to an audience of healthcare professionals. "When I awoke from a coma," he said, "I didn't know that four days had passed since my motorcycle accident. I could not move my arms or legs. I could only move my head. I had some feeling in my lower neck but nowhere else. It wasn't until the next day that I learned I had lost my right leg below the knee as a result of the crushing force of the accident. I was devastated.

When friends came to see me, I was depressed and emotionally withdrawn. I didn't want to face the possibility that I would be a paraplegic stuck in a wheelchair for the rest of my life. And so, one night shortly after a visit from my best friend, I realized that I had a decision to make. Either I would end my life because I could not bear to spend it this way or I would prove the medical experts wrong by walking once again. Thanks to the strong support of my family and best friend, I made the right decision and set short-term goals to recuperate and progress each day."

It was the beginning of a remarkable three-year journey for the former college athlete. Jim worked very hard and eventually recovered feeling and movement in his upper body. With the aid of a brace on his left leg, he regained its partial use and was able to walk from one end of the therapy pool to the other while holding the side railing. His therapy was intense and painful. He devoted four hours every day to rebuilding his muscle strength, re-learning how to walk and riding an exercise bike with a prosthetic leg. In his third year of recovery, Jim began training for a 10K race in his wheelchair. In his fourth year, Jim competed in a half-marathon event for the disabled. It was an exhausting journey, but Jim achieved his goals and now makes a good living as a motivational speaker encouraging others to have faith and never give up.

Jim credits his success in life and business to the nurturing support of his friends and family. But, he also tells his audiences that the decision he made on that lonely night in his hospital bed nearly five years ago was a decision "to live and celebrate the gift of life." From that hospital bed, the former athlete decided to be an athlete once again. Perhaps he would never play professional baseball as he once dreamed, but he would compete again.

However, this time, the opponent wasn't another team or athlete. It was his ego and physical limitations. It was the negative voices inside his head and the opinions of experts who had already decided his fate. Yet, against those odds, Jim summoned the courage to fight those negative voices and reject the collective wisdom of so many highly trained experts. Jim decided to live the new life he had been given and to celebrate the gift of life to its fullest. In doing so, he proved the doubters wrong.

Jim also understood that how he perceived life would make a difference in his ability to either live a life of limitations or achieve his new goals. William Blake, the English poet and visionary mystic, said, "If the doors of perception were cleansed, man would see things as they truly are, infinite." Jim chose to open his doors of perception and embrace all the possibilities.

Jim's use of the phrase "celebrate the gift of life" resonated with me as I continued on my walk. Certainly, there were other remarkable stories similar to his. I began to think about all those people who had suffered from cancer, alcoholism and drug abuse only to recover and lead prosperous lives. They, too, refused to surrender. I thought about hurricane, tornado and tsunami victims who lived through the horror of those natural disasters and were fortunate to be rescued before being swept away by the savage forces of nature. And what can be said about amazing people like Gandhi who gave his life to win independence for his beloved nation of India? Or, Mother Teresa, who nurtured the bodies and spirits of abandoned, homeless people who had been rejected by mainstream society and left to languish in the gutters of Calcutta? They also found a way to *celebrate the gift of life.*

As I walked on, the sun began its slow climb over the Vallecito Mountains to the east of Mt. Woodson. The athlete's story reminded me what *The Course* teaches us about life's irony. The irony of living is that we do not have control over tomorrow but only this moment—right here, right now. Yet, one of the frustrations of living in the moment is that rarely do we know if today's efforts will do any good or result in some positive outcome. You can only set in motion *activities* and hope the results turn out the way you want them to. Although activities are within our span of control, results are not. We can only *influence* results provided we perform the *right* activities.

How do I celebrate the gift of life? I re-read the First Sacred Question on the white card as I climbed the steep cart path along the 12th fairway. The sun felt warm on my back. Suddenly, a rattlesnake startled me as it slithered across the cart path less than ten feet in front of me and disappeared into a pile of rocks that bordered the path. "Whew, that was close," I told myself as my heart pounded quickly! My first reaction had been to defend myself and kill it.

But the snake moved too quickly. In a moment, the rattler had disappeared into the crevice before I could regain my composure and react. I stood there looking into the narrow crack in the rocks where the rattlesnake had crawled. There was no sign of it and I was not about to stick my hand or foot under the rocks to probe its whereabouts. I chuckled nervously to myself realizing this event signified another aspect of the First Sacred Question Ajay had asked me to answer.

Certainly, part of celebrating the gift of life was to respect all living things, not just people. I had the power to hunt down and kill that venomous snake but upon reflection, I realized that it meant no harm to me. In fact, as I thought about it, the pounding reverberations of my feet on the cart path probably alerted the snake to my presence and warned it of my ensuing approach. In a split second, the snake reacted and slithered across the cart path for the safety of the nearby rocks sparing both of us an unpleasant encounter. Had I stepped on it, well, the rattler would have defended itself and bit me; but it knew enough to get out of the way before I came any closer. "How interesting," I thought to myself as I stood there observing the rocks where it had disappeared, "that snake had the instinctive knowledge and skill to avoid human contact so neither one of us was harmed." I walked on keeping a close watch for any of the creepy crawler's relatives that might be basking in the warm morning sun that now soaked the cart path.

As I continued my walk along the green deserted fairways I thought about another aspect of the gift of life. I reflected on people whose lives were cut short as a result of an early death. Ironically, in dying many of them gave life and new hope to others. For example, I read a newspaper story about a college student who had died in a car accident. This young woman enjoyed creative writing and while at college, she encouraged many high school students whom she tutored to pursue their creative writing dreams. After her death, her parents endowed a creative writing center at her alma mater. Although the young woman is deceased, her passion continues through the college's creative writing center. This, too, is a form of celebrating the gift of life.

Also, I recall seeing a bumper sticker encouraging people to donate their organs. It read, "Heaven doesn't need your organs, but heaven knows *we* do." It made me appreciate the Biblical passage, "…and in dying, He gave life to others." What was written 2,000 years ago remains relevant today on so many levels.

Just like Jim, the talented athlete who was given superior talent on the playing field but was disabled in a motorcycle accident, sometimes fate deals us an unkind hand and we must learn to develop new skills and knowledge in order to overcome the adversities of life. I reflected on this scenario and realized that celebrating the gift of life was not only about discovering our skills, knowledge and talent, but also doing something meaningful with them. We cannot all be great athletes or Nobel Prize laureates, but each of us has an important contribution to make in our lifetime. Using our skills, knowledge and talents to discover our higher purpose is part of the key to celebrating the gift of life.

When I returned home, I watched a television program about pet therapy for seniors who were living in assisted care facilities. I thought to myself, "This is interesting. Puppies and kittens are all about giving affection and joy. We pet them, brush them, feed them and they frolic, entertain us, lick us and give us joy." This was yet another aspect of celebrating the gift of life. Newborn babies are the same. They delight us by just being themselves. All they know is love and how to cry when they're hungry or need a diaper changed.

I began to see the logic in the First Sacred Question. In order to connect with my Inner Spirit and discover my higher purpose, I must celebrate the gift of life. But how do I do that? How do I celebrate the gift of life? It was a powerful and provocative question, indeed.

Celebrating the gift of life requires us to take charge and get past the mundane aspects of our day in order to accomplish something significant. Where most people get stuck in life is with the routine stuff. There's no way around it. After all, we must eat, sleep, work, bathe, buy groceries, respond to emails, mow the lawn, wash the car and pay our bills. Yet it's how we respond to life's ordinary tasks that are most important. If we approach the mundane tasks with attention and energy, then they are no longer mundane. If you are attending to life like the great chef who focuses on every detail of a recipe as he prepares an elegant meal, then it moves beyond the mundane and becomes exciting!

There is an old Chinese expression that says: if we wash a tea cup as if it contained the Buddha, we would perform this act with much greater attention and awareness. Every moment in life offers us the opportunity to do things with great attention and love. Redirect your attention when you undertake mundane tasks and try to perform them in the spirit of love and appreciation. Also, what we do in our *spare* time makes a major difference in terms of moving us towards our higher purpose and experiencing a sense of fulfillment. When I answered the First Sacred Question and evaluated how I spent my day, I discovered that I wasted much of my spare time. The challenge was *how* do I choose to spend it?

Success in life happens as a result of focusing on the *vital few* instead of the *trivial many* and having clarity of direction. It's about creating and experiencing your passion and emitting positive energy which comes back to you a thousand fold. If you cannot enjoy "the moment," your life is out of balance. It doesn't matter whether you're writing poetry or playing golf. In order for you to arrive at this basic level of higher consciousness, you must first realize how you see things. *The Course* uses the acronym TWIST, which means, *The Way I See Things*. So, at this early stage, the most important step is to be conscious of *how* you see things. Too often, we just go through life on auto-pilot without ever stopping to ask ourselves questions like, *What am I doing?* or, *Why am I doing this?* or, *If I were to change what I am doing could I create a better outcome?*

We are, by our very nature, creatures of habit. We do the same things day after day mostly because our daily activities are subtle and they become habit-forming. This is part of the Velvet Rut Syndrome which I defined earlier. We get so comfortable with a certain routine that it causes us to stagnate and, eventually, atrophy. To avoid the Velvet Rut, we need new goals and incentives to push us towards our dreams and desires. We also need a dynamic support group—family, friends and colleagues at work—who support our dreams and will encourage us onward. Sometimes, we have a tendency to block out messages of encouragement because we view them as criticism and our ego doesn't like criticism. Once you recognize this point, you can focus on doing positive things and living your passion. This is another key to celebrating the gift of life.

As I struggled with the deeper meaning of the First Sacred Question, I began to appreciate that the only moment I can control is the here and now. All the other variables such as the "who" and "why" don't really matter because they are not under our control. Also, there's no return-on-investment in trying to find fault or blame others for what happened in the past. I learned that I shouldn't spend my time and energy on those things I can't control.

There are millions of people who are searching for life's answers and struggling with this very issue—that is, how do I move beyond something so negative that it keeps me from celebrating life and moving on? It's no coincidence that millions of people are aligned now in thought and action in search of finding significance in their life. The two important questions they are asking themselves are: "Am I living my passion?" and "How can I live a life worth remembering?"

The Course encourages us to practice two exercises to control our thoughts and change them from negative to positive. The first exercise is the *Four-to-One Formula*. This activity will help you think more positive thoughts. We are so programmed to see the negative side of things that most of our reflex thoughts are negative. This, in turn, causes our initial responses and certain behavior to be negative. Negativity has a domino effect on our psyche. It poisons our attitudes and actions while accomplishing nothing worthwhile.

In using the *Four-to-One Formula*, you should think of four positive thoughts for every negative thought that enters your mind. Catch yourself when you realize you are thinking a negative thought even if you never speak it. It could be as trivial as disliking someone's tie or dress, or a negative comment about how your partner drives a car or cursing another driver who doesn't use his turn signal. Practice this exercise for three days by keeping track of *what* you think. When your mind thinks of something negative, immediately challenge yourself to identify four things that are positive. It can be anything related to the situation as long as it's a positive response. You'll be amazed at how often your reflex thoughts are negative.

The Course teaches us that whatever we put out comes back to us. That's why you want to emit joy and positive energy. The Four-to-One Formula will help you replace negative thoughts with positive ones. More importantly, it will help you create peace of mind by giving you greater control over your thoughts. When this happens, your behavior will change. Ultimately, it will result in better outcomes for you because *positive* attracts *positive*!

The second exercise is called *The Sounds of Silence*. This exercise has a dual purpose. It's not that you are trying to control your thoughts as much as you are trying *not* to think. Instead, train your mind to be quiet. Inner peace cannot be achieved amid noise and restlessness. Learn to be still and quiet your mind so you can enjoy a long minute of silence and simply absorb the quiet stillness and powerful energy of silence around you. Consider the silence of nature and the universe. Mother Theresa reminded us that the trees, flowers and grass all grow in silence. The stars, the sun and the moon move in silence. *The Sounds of Silence* is designed to quiet your mind and allow you to live in the moment—the present. By doing this, you will experience peace, serenity and contentment.

Dr. Kavi explained *The Sounds of Silence* this way. When we think, we create too much noise and it is difficult to be present in the moment. But through *The Sounds of Silence* exercise, we quiet the mind, release negative energy and tension and become relaxed. We are peaceful. This allows our positive thoughts to be heard above the clutter of whatever messages our ego is trying to send us.

As I experimented with *The Sounds of Silence* exercise, I remained conscious of my surroundings while releasing all competing thoughts. Just as with meditation or yoga, I simply focused on my breathing—inhaling and exhaling for 60 seconds at a time. This helped me stay in the moment. In the beginning, I found this very difficult to accomplish because the mind registers thousands of thoughts every minute. To limit my mind to just one thought for a few seconds—the act of breathing—seemed nearly impossible. Yet in repeating this exercise many times a day, I eventually learned to experience *the moment*.

Mastering the *Four-to-One Formula* and *The Sounds of Silence* took several days of practice. Eventually, I was able to prevail by changing *what* I think and learning how *not* to think. I simply became present. By changing my thoughts, I was able to change my behavior. By changing my behavior, I was able to modify my attitude. By modifying my attitude, I changed my response to situations. And by changing my response to situations, I created more favorable outcomes. Now I know how to control my thoughts and I have more influence over what I think. While I cannot control outcomes, I can control *how* I respond to events and situations. The response I want to create is one that is peaceful, positive and joyful for me and others.

CHAPTER 12

The Lake Tahoe
Conversation

In September, I flew to Lake Tahoe where I joined Ajay at the Resort at Squaw Creek to address a national business conference and play golf. The September air had turned crisp in the Sierra Nevada Mountains and the autumn colors were abundant as the aspens, cottonwoods and pines splashed the jagged granite mountains with streaks of gold, green and orange.

Ajay and I arrived the day before the conference officially started so we could spend time talking about *The Course* and my progress on the First Sacred Question, *How do I celebrate the gift of life?* We met in the resort's grand lobby lounge in front of the over-sized fireplace where the fire roared to life keeping the sitting room warm from the cool mountain air. We settled into two comfortable leather chairs in front of the fireplace and enjoyed a spectacular view through the floor-to-ceiling windows that framed the faces of Squaw Peak and Granite Chief glistening some 9,000 feet above us. Patches of snow, which remained year-round, could be spotted on the peaks from our perch in the lodge.

Ajay presented me with a gift-wrapped package which I opened. It was a beautiful light brown leather journal. On its cover was an embossed red rose with seven petals and etched underneath it were the words, *A Journal for The Course of 10,000 Days*®. Ajay told me he had a similar journal he used to record his thoughts and observations on *The Course*. He suggested I use mine to make notes, pose questions, record my observations and capture my reflections. Ajay was fond of telling his employees to "ink it as you think it" so good ideas are never forgotten. This is why he always kept a pen and pad of paper by his bed. I opened it to the first blank page and began taking notes as Ajay shared with me his thoughts on the First Sacred Question, *How Do I Celebrate the Gift of Life?*

For two hours, we sat undisturbed in front of the large fireplace drinking herbal tea and discussing the various facets of this intriguing question. After listening to my interpretations and answers, Ajay shared with me Dr. Kavi's thoughts on how we celebrate the gift of life. Dr. Kavi viewed life not only from the perspective of a scientist and physician, but also as a romantic poet. Ajay said, "During *The Course* retreat, we discussed the First Sacred Question and the wonders of life from a human and scientific perspective.

Dr. Kavi explained that in order to truly celebrate the gift of life, it is important to understand exactly what life is. He told us, 'A rational human being wants to understand the source of his being. This is why it's important to seek to understand. We must stretch our minds and stimulate our thinking to a heightened level of curiosity. To accept the wonders of life and our universe on the basis of faith alone is not enough.

While faith can satisfy some of life's mysteries and unanswered questions, human beings should push on for better answers for no other reason than we have the capacity to think, probe, ask questions, debate and decipher information. At the same time, there is a divine connection each person has with the universe and its creator.' Dr. Kavi was fond of Ralph Waldo Emerson's quote that 'each person contains a spark of divinity and it should be found through nature and the deeper exploration of thy own self.' This is an important component of *The Course* and the First Sacred Question."

Ajay sipped his herbal tea and continued. "During *The Course* retreat, Dr. Kavi posed several simple questions that required us to think and explore the complexities of the First Sacred Question. He asked us, 'Why does the bee fly from one flower to the next? Is it because the bee needs the flower, or is it because the flower needs the bee? As you explore the First Sacred Question, hopefully, you will conclude that like the flowers and bees, they need each other. All of life is inter-dependent and, therefore, our very existence is directly tied to all of nature and the farthest reaches of the vast universe including not only what is known to us, but more significantly, what is unknown.'"

Ajay closed his leather journal and added, "When you challenge your mind to move beyond the phase of being awed by the magnificence of life, it's possible to advance to a level of curiosity from which we can explore the intricacies of what makes us function as physical and spiritual beings that think, feel, emote and respond to nature. It is at this level that we begin to understand the awesome power each human being possesses. This is what Dr. Kavi challenged us to do as we contemplated the First Sacred Question—*How do you celebrate the gift of life?*"

Ajay paused as a resort employee tossed two more logs on the fire bringing it to new life, then added, "Another dimension we discussed during the retreat was the irony of life. As physical human beings, we are a composite of both life-giving and life-depleting forces. For example, consider the role of bacteria in our bodies and in the development of our planet. During our retreat, Dr. Kavi explained that bacteria have been on earth for four billion years.

Bacteria comprise about 50 percent of the biomass of the earth and nearly all of its biodiversity. Yet when most people think about bacteria, they think about diseases and germs and not the life-giving forces bacteria possess. For most people, just the thought of bacteria scares us! We're quick to recall our mother's admonition—'go wash your hands!'—so we don't contract some terrible disease like the plague!"

I laughed aloud at Ajay's suggestion because those were the very words my mother had spoken to me countless times when I was a child.

Ajay continued to explain Dr. Kavi's premise about celebrating the gift of life and seeing it through a more complex prism. "Not only do we share our planet with bacteria, we are dependent on them for our survival," he noted. "Studies show that trillions of human cells make up the human body. But, every human body possesses at least ten times that number of bacterial cells. Bacteria coat our skin so we can heal wounds. It lines our intestines so we can digest food and also make vitamins K and B-12. Certain bacteria keep harmful microbes from regenerating and causing illnesses. For each of those positive traits, there is a counter trait whereby bacteria can do harm to our bodies. This is part of what Dr. Kavi conveyed to us as we discussed the yin and yang of life and how we must discover our uniqueness. I share it with you because I want you to appreciate the fact that your gifts and talents will help you unlock the mystery of your higher purpose and allow you to reconnect with your Inner Spirit."

Ajay's was a fascinating dissertation on a level I had never explored before—certainly not in terms of answering a question as penetrating as *How do we celebrate the gift of life?* Ajay's point was to remind me that life is a wondrous thing. And yet, most of us give very little thought as to who we are, how we are made and what are we capable of achieving from a physical, mental, emotional and spiritual dimension. To become fully aware of ourselves requires daily reflection and deep thought. We are living in an era of heightened self-awareness in which more people are taking time each day to meditate, pray and reflect on who they are and what they want to achieve in their lifetime. Ajay's point was that self-awareness isn't something that just happens. It is a conscious action—an ongoing process that requires discipline and focus.

After sharing with me his perspective on the origins of life and how we balance life's positive and negative dimensions such as bacteria, light, time, space and energy, Ajay helped me dissect the First Sacred Question from a philosophical perspective. He told me, "*The Course* teaches us that our existence is not a quirk of faith. We are a vital and intimate part of a higher universe—a universe that has multiple facets including physical, metaphysical and spiritual dimensions. It is our capacity to understand and exist in the metaphysical and spiritual realms that distinguishes human beings from animals. While animals can think and feel, they have no concept of existence, objectivity, property, space, time, causality or possibility thinking. Humans think conceptually. This allows us to function beyond our survival instincts and delight in the exploration of our universe on all levels. Our capacity to think in the spiritual realm is among our greatest gifts along with our ability to pro-create, explore nature and contemplate the Divine Source."

Then Ajay opened his journal again and read a quote he had written down during his retreat weekend in Mumbai. It was from Dr. Richard Moss who authored the book, *The Mandala of Being* (New World Library). "None of us will become our true selves at some fortuitous moment in the future. Our real identities never originate from the remembered glory or trauma of our pasts. It begins anew with the attention we offer to ourselves and to life in each moment."

Ajay sipped his tea and told me, "*The Course* teaches us that part of celebrating the gift of life is to engage in the mystical experience—that intangible realm between science and philosophy where our Inner Spirit dwells and our greatest human powers can be found. If we are truly going to celebrate the gift of life—and not just exist from one day to the next—it's important for us to discover our talents and develop them. It's an ongoing process as Dr. Richard Moss suggests and not something that happens to us in our sleep. We must work at it every day."

This led us to an interesting conversation about the relationship between people and work. I asked Ajay if he considered work to be a process in which we exercise our talent or an obligation we must perform to pay our bills. He reflected on my question and replied, "*The Course* teaches us that work is a means by which we should exercise the best of our talents and skills. Work, in this context, should be rewarding— physically, mentally and financially. Regrettably, many people consider their job to be drudgery. In fact, centuries ago work was associated with a form of punishment. A thousand years ago, if you did not have a craft or trade you were relegated to a life of hardship and, possibly, enslavement. There was little, if any, remuneration or benefit from this type of work. This is how work became associated with punishment. It is no wonder so many people detest getting out of bed on a Monday morning and going off to do a job they hate! This is an unfortunate mind-set. Instead, I would encourage people to consider work from the perspective of Colossians 3:23, which states, "Whatever you do, work at it with all your heart, as working for the Lord, not for men."

The Course reminds us that while most people need to work in order to earn money, today the decision of where we work and the type of work we perform is entirely up to each individual. So, why not work at something you enjoy? Why not engage in some activity or profession that gives you both a sense of satisfaction and generates income? Ajay looked out the window at the mountains above us as the sun begin to disappear behind Squaw Peak and said, "During *The Course* retreat, Dr. Kavi was asked to define *work* and he teased, 'Work is the penalty we pay for not marrying rich!'"

I chuckled at Dr. Kavi's wit as Ajay added, "Too many people are engaged in work that does not fuel their creativity or inspire them to achieve greatness. To some extent I see this even at TGC despite our efforts to help people find fulfillment in their work. It is a sad commentary on today's society that so many people have given up on their dreams and goals and don't exercise their talents and gifts in the workplace. Regrettably, they have settled for a life of quiet desperation and mediocrity. This is not the way one should celebrate the gift of life!"

Before breaking for lunch, Ajay challenged me to reflect on another aspect of the First Sacred Question. He asked me to record in my new journal my response to these questions: What is most important to you? What is it you value more than anything else and want to accomplish? Are you living your life in such a way that helps you achieve that goal or dream? He reminded me that being true to my highest goal and desire will help me to discover my higher purpose.

Ajay's comments were a fitting conclusion to our morning conversation on the First Sacred Question. I began to better understand the complexity of how to celebrate the gift of life and equally important, how to think beyond the obvious in order to appreciate the many blessings, gifts and talents I possessed. After lunch, Ajay and I discussed the three tenets of the First Sacred Question.

CHAPTER 13

The First Tenet of the
First Sacred Question

The three tenets of the First Sacred Question are the supporting legs of an important triad that help us understand how to celebrate the gift of life. At the same time, the three tenets also help us live in the Now and manage our ego.

When we reconvened after lunch, Ajay and I focused on the first tenet: *What are my gifts that make my life unique and special?* Before arriving at Lake Tahoe, I had prepared a list of responses I felt answered the question. For example, I listed such things as my personality, my character, my family, my gift for speaking and writing, my joie de vivre, my love of music and the opportunity to travel. It's fair to say I took my assignment literally.

Since the sun had warmed the fall air, we decided to take advantage of the sunshine and found a table near the outdoor fire pit just off the patio. Ajay opened his brown leather journal and reminded me that our unique gifts and talents are developed as a result of our ability to think, feel, learn and reason. This is the process that leads to wisdom or the realization of truth. The more we develop our mind, the more profound our thinking becomes and, in turn, the greater our gifts and talents are worth. *The Course* teaches that it is through our Inner Spirit that we experience oneness with the universe. This is possible because every human being and living organism is an extension of our universal creator, which *The Course* refers to as the Divine Source.

If this is true, it makes sense that we are a vital part of a system that extends far beyond our planet and solar system—a system that is infinite. It is, in fact, truly universal and without definition. Thus, as quantum physics suggests, we are an extension of the vastness of time and space. Our human energy is derived from the same source as all other energy. Therefore, the potential for human divineness exists because we are made of the same particles and matter as the Divine Source. Human beings have unlimited potential and mental powers. With each new generation, more clues are revealed as to our talents and capabilities. This is why it makes sense that every fiber of our being resonates with the energy of the Divine Source. As life manifest itself in millions of species and organisms—from bacteria to giant redwood trees—the significance of our existence is heightened because we have the power to evolve and attain divine-like attributes. This is evidenced by the fact that throughout recorded history, a handful of human beings exhibited divine traits, most notably Jesus of Nazareth and Buddha.

Carl Jung refers to this state as "the collective unconscious." While some people suggest these super humans were merely undergoing a mystical experience, *The Course* teaches us that every person has the potential to experience human divineness—that state of spiritual bliss that transcends fear and ego needs—and allows us to exist in the breath of the Divine Source through our Inner Spirit. In terms of consciousness, it is that state where our Inner Spirit dominates our thoughts and actions giving us almost supernatural powers. Therefore, it is possible that men like Jesus and Buddha attained such a state and experienced what we commonly refer to today as collective unconscious or divineness.

Throughout the ages, philosophers such as Plato, Archimedes, Socrates, Aristotle and Thomas Aquinas have reinforced this principle. They have spoken and written exhaustively on this subject albeit using different terminology. Poets, authors and mystics have also commented on the plane of reality that lies behind the many dimensions perceptible to our five basic senses. These, too, are references to our human divineness.

For example, Ralph Waldo Emerson asserted, "There is one mind common to all individual men." Ernest Shurtleff Holmes, an American writer and spiritual teacher and the founder of the Religious Science movement, asserted, "There is no such thing as an *individual anything* in the universe." William Blake, the English poet and painter, wrote, "If the doors of perception were cleansed, everything would appear as it is, infinite." Many of the Church's early theologians addressed this important point. For example, during *The Course* retreat, Ajay said that Dr. Kavi cited the work of Thomas Aquinas and traced his writings to Anselm of Canterbury (the Benedictine monk and an early doctor of the Church), then to Augustine of Hippo and finally to Pope Athanasius I of Alexandria. He found a similar thread in all their teachings on the question of human divineness. Aquinas wrote, "God did all things gently and by persuasion in order to gain our trust. Christ became human so that we might become divine."

Thus, what *The Course* advocates with regard to the question of human potential and our ability to reach that level of collective unconscious or divineness is a view that has been corroborated not only by learned men and women throughout the ages, but also theologians and physicists. Scientists have discovered that while reality exists on different levels and that causality—that is, the relationship between causes and effects—is fundamental to all natural science, the ability of the human mind to think beyond the physical realm cannot be measured or limited. Our potential is too great. Therefore, the metaphysical dimensions we are dealing with— including such things as collective unconscious and divineness—are both possible and experiential. Thus, it stands to reason that human beings have experienced such things.

While there are many matters relating to human potential that cannot yet be explained, the fact that questions go unanswered should not devalue or discredit those people who have transcended to higher states of consciousness. As Rumi, the Persian poet and mystic wrote, "Men's minds perceive second causes, but only prophets perceive the action of the first cause."

Given this orientation, Ajay explained how *The Course* refers to a person's talents as their *gifts*. Every person has innate gifts or talents that can be developed over a lifetime. In the process of learning about ourselves, we discover our gifts as well as our passions. Some of the people who found their passion and achieved eminence in their field by shaping the ages with their talents include Sir Isaac Newton, St. Paul, Galileo, Queen Isabella, Columbus, Louis Pasteur, James Watt, Michael Faraday, Michelangelo, Beethoven, Nelson Mandela and Augustus Caesar.

Nevertheless, finding peace is more difficult because your ego is never fully satisfied. There are times when your ego is gratified, but it doesn't last long. Like a drug, once the effect has worn off, the ego is searching for another fix—something else to pursue—all for the illusion of happiness. But happiness doesn't necessarily bring peace. Peace is achieved by finding your authentic self and accepting yourself for who you are. This does not mean you should be satisfied with your imperfections and shortcomings. There is always room for improvement. Accepting yourself for who you are does mean you must take the first step in acknowledging that you are a creation of the Divine Source and can achieve a degree of perfection in this life by allowing your Inner Spirit to lead the way.

This act of accepting yourself is also the first step in loving yourself. When we love something, we want to draw it closer to us. Now this is where the challenge of finding peace in our lives gets difficult. While our ego is at the center of our survival and attends to our physical needs, the ego cannot create peace. Our ego relishes conflict and turmoil. When we live in a state of emotional flux, the ego can maintain control over our emotions and shut out our Inner Spirit. Under these circumstances, it's difficult to know just who we are.

To better understand the First Tenet of the First Sacred Question, *What are my gifts that make my life unique and special?*, *The Course* teaches us that until we can appreciate and acknowledge our gifts and talents, we will remain ignorant of the truth—the truth about our real identity. This means we cannot simply accept our ego's perception of self because it is grossly biased and distorted. Of course, our ego is going to reinforce our best traits and remind us how wonderful we are. This message has been reinforced since we were toddlers. Psychiatrists refer to this perception as the idealized self. And who wouldn't buy into such glowing comments and positive feedback about themselves? This is the very affliction many politicians and dictators suffer from. As *The Course* reminds us, it is in knowing the truth that our authentic self is revealed. Only when our Inner Spirit surfaces to guide us to our higher purpose can we begin to recognize the truth and understand our authentic self.

Socrates suggested that if a man wants to discover the truth he must first get rid of all his opinions. Interestingly, this is the very tactic our ego uses to suppress the truth from us and keep our Inner Spirit at bay. Our ego fills us with opinions instead of facts. The ego substitutes opinions for knowledge and facts and pretends that because we have an opinion we are wise. Confucius said, the authentic self is only known once we "acknowledge the extent of our ignorance."

The Course teaches us that achieving peace requires that you not only know the truth about yourself, but also know what you don't know. In other words, be wise as well as knowledgeable. This leads us to the matter of wisdom. Wisdom is both a process for discovering truth as well as a state of enlightenment that a person attains when truth speaks louder than the ego's deafening voice. It is through wisdom that people are able to achieve their life purpose and live a life of peace and passion. The process of attaining wisdom requires courage because knowing one's gifts is only the first part of the equation. The second part is having the courage to accept those gifts and make the commitment to use them so you can be of service to others. For it is through selfless service that we are able to let go of our imperfections, lies and excuses and live a life based on truth and love. This is why *The Course* asks us to define the gifts that make us unique.

During our discussions at the Resort at Squaw Creek, Ajay explained that he was not interested in the obvious. He already knew those things about me. Instead, he told me that *The Course* was trying to guide me to a higher level of thinking. He wanted me to experience the mental and physical mechanisms necessary to stimulate my mind and control my ego so I could live in the Now. By understanding those mechanisms, I could create unique outcomes in my life. Thus, he counseled, the most important step is to wrestle away control of my mind from the ego and allow my Inner Spirit to guide me to a higher level of consciousness where I can live in the moment.

Frankly, this was a heavy message that required my full concentration and receptiveness. Ajay cautioned me that most people get left behind at this point because they cannot make the leap from ego domination to opening their hearts and minds to allow their Inner Spirit to surface. However, I understood completely what Ajay was telling me because I was struggling to do exactly that. My type A personality would not surrender easily.

Ajay was patient and explained to me how the process works. It required a state of relaxation, breathing calmly and concentrating on a series of simple questions designed to quiet the ego. In the process of undergoing this exercise, I discovered several things. First, I discovered how unrestrained the mind is. Our mind wanders and drifts from thought to thought unless we train it to remain in the present moment. Because our ego struggles with the Now, it resists our efforts to control our thoughts. It fights us by inducing fear and hope and asking "what if" questions. Ironically, while our body functions in the present moment, the mind is free to wander from the present into the past and future. And it does so frequently at the urging of our ego.

I also learned that with practice I could redirect my thoughts from the past and future into the present moment. This was exciting because I learned by using a few simple, repetitive chants that my mind listened to my inner voice and heeded its direction. This process became the vessel by which I could transport my mind from random thoughts and scattered thinking to this moment. In Chapter 30 when I discuss how to create your 100-Day Plan, I will provide you with several chants and tell you how to use this process to redirect your thoughts and behavior.

The Course also teaches us that until we can control our mind and focus on developing our unique talents, we will not be able to live in the moment. Thus, our primary challenge in order to live in the Now is to control the ego because the ego dominates our mind and promotes what *The Course* refers to as "spastic thinking patterns" whereby our mind randomly jumps all over the place—from the present to the future to the past. Such thought patterns are the result of years of un-conditioning.

Without the presence of our Inner Spirit, our ego is free to run amuck and create millions of emotionally-charged images in our mind. While most of those images are positive, a significant number play on our fears, insecurities and vulnerabilities. And our mind is both receptive and responsive to those images—for better or for worse by capturing and recording them without questioning the source or their validity.

An undisciplined mind is like a spinning top that whizzes across the floor without a specific pattern, goal or target. When the spinning top runs out of energy, it keels over and stops. Like the spinning top analogy, we exhaust our mental energies by allowing our mind to drift into the past or race into the future without selectively guiding its thoughts. The more frequently our mind drifts away from the present, the more difficult it is to stay focused on the present and live in the here-and-now. In turn, it's very difficult for most people to explore their unique gifts and discover their higher purpose when the mind is not present in the moment. As I began to understand the reasons for controlling my thoughts, I also began to understand the importance of quieting my ego and, in turn, allowing my Inner Spirit to surface and guide me.

When my mind wandered off into the past, my thoughts were diluted with memories, guilt, nostalgia and regret. When my mind drifted into the future, my thoughts were dominated by matters of hope as well as all the "what if" questions I asked myself. As I became more conscious of my thought patterns, I realized how much time I wasted on the past and future—two places I could not control.

Those people who are commonly referred to as *worry warts* can often be found asking "what if" questions and creating problems before they ever happen. For the worry warts of the world milk and honey equate to calories and cholesterol! Ajay said that worrying is like paying interest on a debt you may never owe. This is but one more reason why it's important to discipline the mind—to remain in the present moment and not allow our mind to consume itself with past issues or future speculation. This is the response Ajay was seeking from me relating to the first tenet. Unfortunately, I was not at a level of consciousness where I could truthfully answer the first tenet of the First Sacred Question. And so, I grappled with meaningful responses as I answered *What are my gifts that make my life unique and special?*

To think on such an enlightened level is very difficult for most people. Why is that? Because our mind is untrained! *The Course* recognizes this flaw in people's thinking patterns and works to teach us how to control our thoughts, stay focused in the Now and fully experience the very moment we are living. At first, these *awareness* exercises were awkward to perform and difficult for me to understand because my ego fought me as I struggled to control my mind. Eventually, through repetition of the exercises and mastering the processes described earlier, I began to gain the upper hand. Also, I realized that an untrained and undisciplined mind was like that spinning top! If I didn't act to control my thoughts and live in the Now, I would never fully come to know and appreciate my unique talents.

While I found all of this Mind-Body-Spirit theory and practice very interesting and helpful, my ego simply wanted to know the answer to the first tenet without doing the pre-work. When I discussed this with Ajay, he told me I reminded him of the child whose mother had read the child's favorite fairy tale at bedtime many times before. Now, the only thing the child wanted to hear was the happy ending. *Tell me the answer*! Of course, he was right. Instead of mastering the process so I could experience the moment and learn for myself, I wanted the Cliff Notes version.

My ego wanted to short-circuit the learning process and get to the answers. So, Ajay humored me with a long story. It was the story of me and my life. He took me back to the beginning of my life so I could explore my Discovery Years and Fulfillment Years and how I had arrived at this point. His goal was to make me fully aware of who I really was as opposed to my ego's interpretation of myself. This meant getting past all the misperceptions and *me-isms* that my ego had filled my mind with over the past 45 years as part of its self-aggrandizement campaign to portray me as Mr. Wonderful.

Ajay cautioned that this process was not meant to discredit me or tear me down—in fact, just the opposite. It was a proven method used by *The Course* to help reaffirm our true self and make us fully aware of our character strengths and flaws, raw emotions, gifts and talents. In this way, we could honestly answer the first tenet of the First Sacred Question, *What are my gifts that make my life unique and special?*

Ajay began this process by quoting the Bhagavan Sri Ramana Maharshi, the enlightened Indian sage from the 19th century who said, "To truly know one's self, you must go back by the way that you have come." Ramana Maharshi also counseled, "If we trace the source of 'I' thought (or Me-ism), then our ego starts disappearing and our true Self is revealed."

One of the teachings of the Bhagavan Sri Ramana Maharshi that *The Course* embraces deals with the subject of Awareness. The Indian sage believed we are awareness. He said, "Awareness is another name for you. Since you are awareness there is no need to attain or cultivate it. All that you have to do is to give up being aware of other things. If one gives up being aware of other things, then pure awareness alone remains; and that is the [true] Self."

As Ajay explained these things to me and helped me replay critical events and transitional moments in my life, I began to form a clearer picture in my mind of who I was and how I became the person sitting there in front of that warm fireplace on a cool autumn afternoon at the Resort at Squaw Creek. It was a powerful moment—coming to understand and appreciate myself for who I really was—my character strengths and flaws, my emotions and talents. At that moment, I experienced a heightened sense of awareness as a unique human being who was less than perfect, but one with unique gifts who was living a life worth remembering.

Oddly enough, I was not threatened by that experience or what I revealed about myself to Ajay. There was no effort on the part of my ego to defend my inadequacies or faults or to trumpet my accomplishments. It was a peaceful, cleansing moment for me as I responded to Ajay's questions. For his part, Ajay offered no advice, made no judgments, nor did he suggest any comments that might hint of acceptance or disapproval. It was simply a time of reflection, acknowledgment of my past and the realization that I was fully in the moment and aware of my true self.

Before taking a break from our discussions, Ajay shared with me another quote from the Bhagavan Sri Ramana Maharshi because of its relevance to our topic. Ramana Maharshi said, "The state we call realization is simply being oneself, not knowing anything or becoming anything. If one has realized, he is that which alone is, and which alone has always been. He cannot describe that state. He can only be that."

As I completed more of *The Course* exercises and responded to the Three Sacred Questions, I realized the linkage between my ego, my mind and my thoughts in connection to life's outcomes. The more aware I became of my mind's habit to drift into the past or future, the faster I learned to pause briefly, stop thinking, recite the chants that Ajay had taught me from *The Course* and bring my mind back to the present moment so I could live in the Now. This is how I learned to control my thoughts and live in the moment.

The benefit of living and thinking in the Now is simple: you experience life to the fullest and enjoy its pleasures. You are completely alive and engaged in the experience of whatever you are doing. You miss nothing. Your mind and body are in sync as you embrace each moment. Your emotions are genuine and not corrupted by the past or future. And most importantly, you do not live in fear.

When we continued our conversation, Ajay told me he wanted to share some thoughts on the subject of fear and how it can hold us back from celebrating the gift of life and using our unique gifts. *The Course* teaches us that too often we enable fear by allowing it to take us where it wants—to a place deep within our mind where the ego can hide from reality and feel safe against whatever threats are causing it to cower. As I learned, if we can use our special talents to confront our fears, which we all have, more often than not we can successfully dissect those fears and conquer them.

Ajay reminded me of the power of words to alter one's perception as a way to overcome fear. An example of this was Franklin D. Roosevelt's first Inaugural Address on March 4, 1933 when he spoke these remarkable words: "The only thing we have to fear is fear itself." In those ten words, President Roosevelt re-energized the American people and awakened their spirit. According to Adam Cohen in his insightful book *Nothing to Fear* (Penguin Press), it was as if Roosevelt had lifted a huge boulder off the shoulders of the American people and inspired them to boldness with his call for "action, and action now." My late father, who lived through the Depression, told me it was at that moment that the American people began to believe they could overcome their hardships and accomplish whatever was required to pull the nation out of the Depression. Roosevelt had transformed America's worse fears into hope.

Fear is a paralyzing emotion and psychological state of mind. It can hold us back when we should act and cause us to miss great moments of opportunity. I feel for those people who cannot enjoy a Caribbean cruise because they don't know how to swim and fear drowning if the ship goes down. I also feel for those folks who will never see the world because they're afraid to fly. I know this to be true because years ago I used to be a white-knuckled flier. Eventually, I was able to overcome my fear using several exercises that coincidentally are also taught in *The Course*.

Many people live in fear because their minds are racing into the future and asking fear-based "what if" questions like "What if the engines fail and we crash?" or "What if we hit an iceberg and sink?" and "How will I survive?" Their need for control is so strong they cannot surrender control to the airline pilot or ship's crew. Instead, their ego convinces them not to fly or cruise. It's silly, but so true and very real for too many people.

Sometimes, our survival and security instincts are so intense they cause our mind to play wild games on us to the point where we imagine our worst fears coming true. By understanding how to place our trust in others, we can relax and live in the moment. It also helps if we can appreciate our talents. For example, everyone can swim. Even dogs and horses can swim!

It's just a matter of keeping your mouth closed so water doesn't fill-up your lungs and using your arms and legs in a coordinated fashion to paddle and stay afloat. It's almost second nature for most people and animals!

Over time, we learn to not only survive, but also how to thrive in difficult situations! Human resilience is amazing. Our survival instincts can be a very positive thing provided we don't panic and allow our mind to run wild with fear-based, irrational thoughts. In the case of those white-knuckled fliers or non-swimmers on a cruise ship, it helps to stay in the moment and know the pilot is skilled, experienced and trained in emergency tactics while cruise ships have sophisticated navigation equipment aboard to help them steer through stormy seas and avoid icebergs. And, don't forget, every ship has extra life boats and a trained crew. Knowing this, the rational person should be able to sit back, relax and enjoy their trip. No fear!

Ironically, fearing the consequences of our actions can be a good thing because it prevents us from doing something we will regret later—like having another drink or cheating on our income taxes. This is our Inner Spirit's way of reminding us it's not worth it!

What *The Course* reminds us about dealing with fear is this: Each of us has the power to resist fear and transform our fears into a new reality. That reality is based on self-compassion because we have suffered. It is based on acknowledging that a new day brings hope because fear should not be our overlord. It is based on our ability to overcome self doubts because we have done so hundreds of times before in little ways. Most significantly, that reality is based on love—the love our Inner Spirit and ego feel for us and the love others have for us. We are not alone even in our darkest moments. We have a vast network of people who genuinely care about our well-being and happiness. They want to help us if we will only reach out to them. Too often, our ego tries to hold us back from reaching out to others for help. The ego uses pride as a way to keep us from making that phone call or texting a friend in our hour of need. It is in these special moments that we need to summon our Inner Spirit and seek its guidance and help. The good news is our Inner Spirit will *always* respond. It always heeds the call and will never fail us, yet we must ask it to come forward and be present in our life at that moment. More often than not, this is all we need to do to help us overcome our fears and reach a higher level of awareness so we can live in the Now. This is how we escape the clutches of fear—by supplanting it with love and the presence of our Inner Spirit.

That evening, I decided to have an early dinner at the Ristorante Montagna. I brought along my journal and sat at a table in a quiet corner and began to make notes about the three tenets as I enjoyed a glass of the Toad Hallow Pinot Noir wine which the waiter highly recommended. I reflected on my day-long conversations with Ajay while I ate dinner. So much good food and wine made me drowsy. But the crisp mountain air reinvigorated me as I made my way back to the main lodge along the outdoor pathway.

The sun had set and the stars were ablaze in the sky as I inhaled the chilly night air. Once inside the main building, I returned to the place where Ajay and I had spent the better part of the morning and got comfortable in a large chair near the glowing fireplace. There I settled down to enjoy my wine and review my notes in preparation for my morning speech and a follow-up meeting with Ajay. After nearly two hours, I decided to go to bed. A full moon hovered over the northwestern peaks surrounding the resort. Its pale blue light guided me down the outdoor path to my building past the heated Jacuzzi where a few diehard easterners were enjoying the hot tub to ward off the cold mountain air. "Not tonight," I said to myself as I climbed the stairs to my guest room on the third floor to stretch my leg muscles. Then I settled in for a good night's sleep.

CHAPTER 14

The Second Tenet of the First Sacred Question

The second tenet is *How do I share my gifts with others?* It occurred to me that the gift of life would not be possible without the most basic things we take for granted. For example, the gift of life requires natural resources such as air, trees, plants, rivers and streams. It requires rain, the forests and thousands of ecological systems that sustain our planet. All of these wonders are essential to our existence.

While I reflected on my responses, I recalled a principle *The Course* refers to as *Givers Gain*. What *Givers Gain* means is that we should always give more than is expected of us and, in turn, we will receive more. Kindness and service to others are at the core of this tenet. In my effort to connect the dots between kindness, service and giving, I concluded that the degree to which we are able to celebrate life is in direct proportion to how much we give of ourselves to others.

Ajay told me of an axiom that Dr. Kavi liked to quote about giving. It goes, "A gift comes from your wallet, but a sacrifice comes from your heart." It caused me to consider how I shared my gifts with others. I realized that my time and physical presence were more important than just my money.

In order to give your life meaning, you must acknowledge that you are part of something greater than just yourself. This is why we must have respect for all living things. We are connected to everything and everyone. This is the significance of the First Sacred Question. In the grand design of the universe, there is more to consider than just you or me. This is the significance of our world—it can exist without us, but we cannot exist without it.

In an ego-driven society we are seduced into thinking "it's all about me." But, it's not. This type of self-centered thinking devalues life and distorts our role in the universal order. However, when you view your life as part of the Divine Source's master plan, and see it in relation to everything else that exists on our planet and throughout our universe, it gives your life greater significance and value. That is why human beings need to appreciate all other living things on our planet. To do otherwise is to diminish the worth of our own life and existence.

Another important lesson is that it's impossible to acknowledge the existence of your Inner Spirit if you don't respect all living things. *The Course* teaches us that all life is sacred. This is why capital punishment is morally wrong. It devalues life. Our Inner Spirit is not some mysterious entity that operates alone. It draws its energy and sustenance from other human beings as well as all forms of life in this universe. I'm referring to the wind, water and heavens. I'm referring to the energy other people emit as well as the energy produced by our Inner Spirit. What is also profound is that our Inner Spirit draws energy and inspiration from the Inner Spirits of those who have died because their spirits live on.

As you study *The Course* and come to understand the power of your Inner Spirit, you will learn that while people physically live and die, your Inner Spirit lives on in the metaphysical and spiritual worlds. It continues to draw energy and strength and communicates at a much higher level of consciousness. This is a universal truth that has been known since the days of Socrates.

The Course teaches us that the Divine Source is fully aware of each human being through their Inner Spirit and responds to our prayers if communicated through the proper channel. This is why we must study the process of how to direct our prayers. Our prayers and desires must be sent not through a human channel, but through a spiritual channel. And that conduit is our Inner Spirit. Studying how to direct our energies and thoughts through our Inner Spirit is an important component of *The Course*. Knowing how to direct our spiritual communications to the Divine Source is essential for tapping into our divine powers. As Karl Barth reminds us, "Prayer without study would be empty, and study without prayer would be blind."

As Ajay and I discussed the second tenet of the First Sacred Question— *How do I share my gifts with others?*—he reminded me that sharing our gifts with others requires much more than performing random acts of kindness. In fact, what *The Course* teaches us is that sharing our gifts is part of our authenticity. It works this way. Your Inner Spirit wants to participate completely in your life. But, too often, your ego slams the door and locks the Inner Spirit out by masquerading as something you are not. It's part of human nature to want to appear more important and relevant than we actually are at any moment. I suppose this is why some people lie on their resumes or overstate their life accomplishments. This is simply the ego's response to insecurity and the fear of rejection.

Our ego tries to mask our ineptness and fake it. Contrarily, our Inner Spirit has no such insecurities because it understands that we have the potential to achieve divineness as human beings just as Jesus did; therefore, it accepts us for who we are at *this* very moment. Ironically, our ego struggles with this notion of acceptance because the ego cannot deal with our imperfections. This is why our ego fabricates lies and schemes—to inflate our self-worth so it can create an illusion and trick our brain into believing we are better, smarter, richer or more successful than we really are. It is all a charade on the part of the ego to boost our self-importance. Most people recover from these occasional delusions of grandeur or ego fantasies. However, there are people who become so entangled in this hallucination of the ego that they lose touch with reality and require psychiatric treatment. This, in part, explains why people escape reality by abusing alcohol and drugs.

Another important aspect of the Second Tenet is knowing the types of gifts we possess. Each person enjoys two types of gifts. The first are Natural Gifts. For example, you might have a natural talent as a creative writer, scientist, musician, athlete or mathematician. These are gifts we acquire through the mental triad of skills, knowledge and talent. The second type of gifts are those Supernatural Gifts which we develop through our Inner Spirit. For example, I have met people who are spiritual healers and clairvoyants. Only someone who is connected to their Inner Spirit is capable of accessing their supernatural gifts.

Your Inner Spirit will always guide you down the right path. And, if you ask your Inner Spirit to reveal the truth, it will. Now, here is the most powerful secret of *The Course*. Your Inner Spirit knows the answers to your most pressing questions about life. I'm talking about questions like "What is my higher purpose?" or "How can I achieve my goals?" It also knows where you want to go professionally and personally, and how to get you there. I'm referring to matters of the heart as well as applying your talents and skills to achieve professional success. However, you must be in control of your life. Your Inner Spirit has amazing powers and while it knows your destiny, it cannot control your choices. The reason your Inner Spirit knows your destiny is because it possesses a sixth sense type of power and wisdom.

The Course defines destiny as that metaphysical dimension in which your seven chakras align with your Inner Spirit to guide you down the path you have chosen for your life. With each decision you make, your destiny is revealed. However, whenever you ignore your Inner Spirit or listen only to your ego, your destiny can be adversely affected.

While you can attempt to realign your seven chakras with your Inner Spirit, often times you will end up on a new path that leads you in a different direction. It is simply a matter of the decisions you make. As *The Course* teaches us, there are choices and consequences for every decision we make—some for better and some for worse.

Sometimes we fail to recognize the voice of our Inner Spirit and in those moments we fail to benefit from its counsel. Sometimes our ego clouds our thinking and judgment. In those instances, we allow our ego to take us back to the safety and comfort of our past instead of spreading our wings and venturing towards our dreams and goals. But when you seek its intervention, your Inner Spirit will surface and guide you towards your destiny. When this happens, it is important that you know your talents, apply them and not abandon your dreams.

Over the past several years, I've carefully pondered the existence of the Divine Source and reflected on my relationship with my Inner Spirit. Dr. Kavi told me that Albert Einstein and Professor Stephen Hawking, undisputedly two of the greatest scientific minds of our time, taught their students to think beyond the obvious and challenge the status quo. This includes the realm of metaphysics. When Dr. Kavi reminded me of Einstein's approach to the universe and his acceptance of similar principles, it opened my mind to new possibilities.

Like Dr. Kavi, I came to the realization that science can only answer what is known and tested. But there is another powerful realm—the metaphysical realm where spiritualism, faith and human divineness exist on different levels of reality. I have no doubt that while the metaphysical realm is grossly misunderstood and undervalued, it is real. I think this is what Professor Hawking meant when he told *Der Spiegel* magazine in 1989, "We are just an advanced breed of monkeys on a minor planet of a very average star. But, we can understand the Universe and that makes us something very special."

Our Inner Spirit controls our spiritual dimension which deals with our soul, destiny and eternal life. One of the great mysteries of life—and frustrations for those who have been schooled in the sciences—is that this spiritual realm cannot be explained by the kind of science that is practiced today. It is too advanced and sophisticated.

Thomas Aquinas, who lived in the 13th century and is considered one of the greatest philosophers and theologians of the Catholic Church, wrote extensively about this matter and concluded that such unresolved questions form the basis of one's faith. This is what I have come to accept. Without the benefit of personal experience, faith is required to embrace the concept of the Divine Source or some power greater than ourselves. It is also necessary if we are to believe in our divine potential as human beings. This awakening was the beginning of my spiritual transformation and the key that eventually unlocked the door to my Inner Spirit.

I was like so many people in their 40s and 50s. I was unknowingly and unwittingly controlled by my ego. Once I started to think deeply about what was going on in my life and why I was not more fulfilled spiritually, I began to challenge certain assumptions. I began to think. My ego fought me along the way in an effort to maintain control. It was at this point I realized I was not celebrating the *here and now* or living in the moment.

Looking back, I can understand why this was a scary process for my ego. After all, my ego had never completely trusted anyone before and I had never placed my faith and trust in a higher power. But once I took the first step and allowed my Inner Spirit to surface, my life changed for the better. Good things began to happen. This has been my experience since I learned to listen to my Inner Spirit and allow it to guide me through my Legacy Years.

Ajay told me a story about the power of destiny and how it can be activated when we listen to our Inner Spirit. His next door neighbor is a gentleman named Albert. Forty years ago, Albert walked into Dayton's department store in Minneapolis late one Friday afternoon to buy a birthday gift for his sister whom he was visiting for the weekend. In the store, Albert was helped by a lovely single woman named Martha who was working overtime because her co-worker had called in sick. Albert started a conversation with Martha. That conversation led to a cup of coffee and a year later, Albert and Martha were married. That was 39 years ago. They are still very much in love and have four children and six grandchildren!

It wasn't a freak occurrence. It happens thousands of times every day all over the world because people pause long enough to allow their Inner Spirit to speak and be heard. When we do this, our seven chakras come into alignment and wonderful things happen. One of those is what we commonly refer to as the Law of Attraction.

I asked Ajay how he would respond to critics who claim such occurrences are simply coincidences and part of what happens in life. "I cannot argue the point," Ajay replied. "It can be doubted, but it cannot be disputed. You see, I know what I know and my convictions are stronger than anyone's doubts. People will believe whatever they want to believe. But whenever I meet someone who dismisses these occurrences as coincidences, I ask them three questions:

1. Do you believe there is a grand design for our universe?
2. Do you believe that you are here on earth without guidance from a higher power? Or do you believe in a higher power whether that higher power resides within you or outside of you and guides you to your destiny?
3. Do you believe that your life is merely circumstantial and has no relationship or connectivity to anything else in the universe? Or, do

you believe in connectedness? And if you believe in connectedness, where does that connectedness start and end?"

When I first learned these questions, it led me to the realization that life is much greater than any one individual. Ultimately, the enlightened mind will ask the question, *Where is the Divine Source not?*

CHAPTER 15

The Third Tenet of the First Sacred Question

T he third tenet of the First Sacred Question is *How do I use my gifts to create a better life for myself and others?* This was the final topic of conversation Ajay and I discussed that afternoon at Lake Tahoe. Ajay reminded me that life can only be enjoyed or celebrated by people who put aside their problems, stop worrying and live in the moment. He asked me if I appreciated the simple gifts of life, for example, a new day, a full moon, the beautiful celestial colors of a sunrise and sunset and the changing colors of autumn leaves.

I have met people who always see the glass as half empty. They pine away their days begrudging the fact that their neighbors have a nicer lawn, or their co-workers make more money, have newer cars and travel to exotic getaway places on the weekends. For some reason, these people attract pain and suffering into their lives. They wallow in self-pity and some of these people actually seem to enjoy being unhappy. It gives them something to complain about and makes them the center of attention. Their condition reminds me of the Zen aphorism that goes, "Pain is inevitable, but suffering is optional."

I have also met many over-achievers who never stopped long enough to smell the roses. For them, life was a blur of meetings, goals, budgets, analyzing stock prices, responding to emails, forecasting revenue and performance, new product launches, retirement parties and then, suddenly, emptiness and loneliness. By the time these over-achievers reach retirement age, they are spent. They have little energy to do anything significant and few close friends. They have given their *all* to the company and now there is nothing to fill the void in their life.

I often remind my seminar audiences about the importance of enjoying the journey. On the subject of living a life worth remembering, I tell them, "I don't know about you, but when I'm dead and gone, I hope they have something more profound to etch on my tombstone than 'Tom Made Budget!'" While that one-liner always draws a big laugh, there is an important message hidden within the humor. Don't wait until it's too late to live your life and make a difference.

In a poem entitled *A Prayer for Today*, Dr. Heartsill Wilson writes:

> *But what I do today is important because*
> *I am exchanging a day of my life for it.*

Perhaps this is what Ajay meant when he told me that life was not about how quickly you reached your destination, but how much of the journey you remembered and celebrated along the way. Achieving that inner sense of peace and contentment is part of the key to how we will be remembered. This is why *The Course* asks us the question, "What is the legacy I want to create for myself?" To answer it, we must start with our desired result then design our life from that perspective.

If you are not at peace with yourself or satisfied with your results thus far, it's difficult to fully celebrate your gifts. Such conditions cause stress and discontent in our lives. The more I thought about this simple premise, the more I began to appreciate the need for my Inner Spirit to be heard.

The Course also teaches us that every human being has the ability to create a better life. But our ego constantly challenges us by suggesting we are not good enough or our talents are inadequate to do the job. I recall Ajay telling me how Buddha was once an ordinary man before he discovered his true gift as a teacher and celebrated his life by sharing his wisdom with others. This young man, who was born into royalty in 624 BC, was named Siddhartha. Despite his father's plans for Siddhartha to succeed him, the young man's life took a very different path. He gave up his royal life to live with the Brahmans who taught him for several years. Eventually, Siddhartha came to realize his gifts. For 45 years, Buddha (meaning "The Awakened One") taught the Four Noble Truths and today 2500 years later, the influence of Buddha is greater than ever before.

What is interesting about Buddha is that to his followers he is neither a god, nor a divine incarnation. Nor is he a prophet bearing a message of divine revelation. Buddha is merely a human being who, by his own striving and intelligence, reached the highest spiritual attainment of which man is capable—perfect wisdom, full enlightenment and the complete purification of the mind. His self-less service to humanity was that of a teacher—a world teacher—who, out of compassion, showed the way for others so that we might also discover our higher purpose and achieve full enlightenment.

Ajay told me the third tenet challenges us to move beyond our selfish needs and consider the impact we have on others as well as our connectedness to all living things. So, how can we expedite this introspective process to help us better use our gifts and talents? There are two proverbs that speak to the third tenet. The first is "Every seed knows its time." The second is attributed to the Chinese philosopher, Lao Tsu, who said, "When the student is ready the teacher will appear." These proverbs are consistent with the first and fourth laws of the Seven Laws of the Universe.[1]

For the child prodigy, his or her gifts are obvious. They effortlessly excel at their calling. But for the remaining 99% of us, we must jumpstart that process. *The Course* suggests three ways to do this. First, pay attention to what you enjoy doing with your time. If you enjoy playing the piano, perhaps you have a gift to compose music. If you enjoy crossword puzzles or playing chess, that could be a sign of your ability to solve problems. If you are an outstanding basketball player, perhaps you are a gifted athlete. Parents should closely observe their children and encourage them to pursue those activities in which their children have an interest or talent.

The second thing is to experiment. Be open to innovation and new ideas like the famous Los Angeles chef who told me he had never set foot in a kitchen to cook a meal until he was 33 years old. Then, one day, he helped a friend prepare a recipe and he was hooked! He quit his day job and studied to become a chef. Today, he owns four profitable restaurants in Southern California.

Finally, be focused and disciplined. Once you find your passion, you need to work at it each day to become the best in your field. This is true of every profession. Be the best house painter. Be the best gardener. Strive to be the best plumber, auto mechanic, teacher, concert pianist or accountant. Whatever your talents, master them!

But to be at our best requires our ego to be supportive of our goals. It requires us to overcome self doubts and limitations knowing we have the necessary talents or gifts to achieve greatness. There are people who possess great talent but never blossom or succeed partly because of self-doubt and missed opportunities. Certainly, there is another Picasso, Hemingway, Elvis or Churchill in the world who has just as much talent, but, because of one missed opportunity or self-doubt, is never discovered. Too often, that one missed opportunity or momentary hesitation can derail our rendezvous with destiny and success. Some of our doubts and limitations are the result of negative messages that were programmed into our mind while we were impressionable children.

Fortunately, our Inner Spirit does not deal in negativity or limitations. It deals in possibilities and creating positive outcomes. Only our ego internalizes negative images and programming. Over a lifetime, our ego comes to believe many of the negative messages we learned. This is unfortunate because most of them are lies or destructive communications taught to us by people who were angry or vengeful. As Kavi told me, "The people who love each other the most also betray each other the most."

The Course teaches us to accept not only who we *are*, but also who we *want* to become. When I realized this significant point, it freed my mind and allowed me to think on a different wavelength. At that moment, I realized I did not have to be limited to a certain personality type just because I was driven and goal-oriented. I also realized I did not have to be confrontational, combative or argumentative with people in order to make my voice heard or have my way. Over time, I learned that other approaches—kinder, compassionate and loving approaches—actually work better with most people. As a result of studying *The Course* and living in a more enlightened state, I changed. I gradually moved closer to becoming the person I wanted to be.

After completing the first phase of *The Course* and understanding myself better, I was able to objectively re-evaluate whether or not I was pleased or displeased with certain aspects of my behavior and personality. It was not a question of whether I was a good person or a competent person; rather, I learned to evaluate what was working in my life and what I needed to change in order to achieve my higher purpose.

I also learned that for me to change those things about myself I did not like, I had to accept two important premises that are consistent with the second and third tenets of the First Sacred Question. First, I had to accept the Divine Source. By embracing this core belief, I validated my life and its higher purpose. To not accept the existence of the Divine Source is akin to thinking I am living a life that has no meaning or purpose beyond my existence. If that's the case, having a higher purpose is irrelevant. This premise follows the same argument Socrates made in Plato's famous story, *The Phaedo*. I discuss this issue in more detail during the third phase of *The Course*, Acceptance of the Divine.

Secondly, I accepted the premise that I am a unique human being who is capable of achieving extraordinary things because I am on this earth as a result of the Divine Source's grand plan. My life is not a mistake nor is it some random act. My existence is part of the grand design of our universe. Like a grain of sand on the beach, I contribute to the whole of the universe. I matter. My life is significant.

Through *The Course*, I learned how to access the potent powers of my Inner Spirit and change my behavior. Another powerful exercise I learned—The Three W's—asks me to answer three questions related to the First Sacred Question. They are:

1. What is going right in my life?

2. What is out of balance in my life?

3. What am I prepared to change *today* in order to achieve the balance and happiness I want to create in my life?

What I like about the third question is that it ties together the Three W's exercise and forces me to either take action or continue to live in pain and discontent. These questions force me to confront the man in the mirror. I must acknowledge *who* I am at this moment and *where* I am in my life right now. It also challenges me to set life goals and prioritize what is important to me. This is something only I can do. No one else can answer these questions for me because they are an essential part of the Acceptance of Self phase of *The Course*.

The Course teaches us that life is a sacred journey—a circuitous route that is designed to take us from a state of perfection at birth to a state of completion when we experience our physical death. And hopefully, this journey makes us whole as a person. This is how we live a life worth remembering.

The French philosopher Gabriel Marcel said, "Life is a meandering through mystery." The mystery that *The Course* unlocked for me was my relationship with my Inner Spirit and my ability to connect with the Divine Source. I meandered through life for 45 years. But after I was introduced to *The Course*, I found a path that helped me discover my higher purpose and create peace and passion in my life.

CHAPTER 16

The Second Sacred Question

I returned to San Diego after a successful trip to Squaw Valley focused on answering the Second Sacred Question. *Have you forgiven those who have offended you? And, have you asked for forgiveness from those you have offended?* It was a difficult question that required me to probe deep into my past and revisit many instances and encounters that were not pleasant.

In keeping with my practice of entering each new day by reading something inspirational and uplifting, the next day I selected a passage related to *The Second Sacred Question* by the Buddhist teacher, Ajahn Chah:

If you let go a little, you will have a little happiness.
If you let go a lot, you will have a lot of happiness.
If you let go completely, you will be free.

I also read a verse from *The Book of Daily Course Inspirations*. This is an insightful book Dr. Kavi compiled and edited from various readings and teachings over a 25-year period. The verse I read that day was from the late Catholic Archbishop Fulton J. Sheen of Baltimore who wrote, "The real test of a Christian is not how much he loves his friends, but how much he loves his enemies." It was a fitting start to a new day—a day that would take me further down the path of Forgiveness.

A chill was in the mid-September air at Mt. Woodson so I donned a sweater to keep warm. I picked up my shillelagh, which had been given to me by my late uncle, Jim Walsh. From time to time, I carried this rough-looking walking stick with me to snag a golf ball or defend myself against various critters in the early morning hours. As I walked along the lush fairways of Mt. Woodson golf course, I recalled the story of this particular shillelagh and how my late Uncle Jim came to possess it. He told me he found it near the Shillelagh Forest in County Wicklow, Ireland where he visited while stationed with the U.S. Army Air Force in England during World War II.

With my shillelagh in hand, I made my way around the golf course walking around the back nine holes where no golfers would be playing at this early hour of the morning. I allowed my mind to drift in thought and, eventually, somewhere around the 11th hole, I thought about The Second Sacred Question and its three tenets.

I pulled the white business card that Ajay gave me at Las Brisas restaurant from my pants pocket and read it. The three tenets of the Second Sacred Question are:

Have you forgiven yourself for past mistakes and wrongdoings?
Have you forgiven others for offending you and hurting you?
What are you doing today to take ownership of your life?

As I walked along the cart path that curved through the thick scrub oak trees and crossed over a narrow bridge, I reflected for a moment on the first tenet, *Forgiveness of Self*. *The Course* reminds us that people create their own hell on earth by making poor decisions and never forgiving themselves for their stupidity. *The Course* defines Hell as a subconscious state that people create in their minds to deal with the absence of love, compassion and forgiveness. It is also that void within us where we are physically and spiritually separated from the Divine Source because we are unable to forgive, and therefore, unable to give or receive love.

Hell is also that physical and mental state where we suffer the pain, loneliness and torment of our wrongs against others. Hell is that space in time where a person's life is suspended indefinitely because they refuse to acknowledge or hear their Inner Spirit. When our Inner Spirit surfaces, we can escape the pains of hell because Forgiveness is possible; and the act of forgiving ourselves and others requires us to let go of the negative emotional experience and guilt. In order for someone to let go they must change *how* they think. This transformation of thought requires us to summon our Inner Spirit because only our Inner Spirit can open our hearts to the point where we are willing to acknowledge our mistakes, have compassion for ourselves, atone for any wrongs we've committed and reconcile our ways.

The ego does not engage in forgiveness. Instead, the ego thrives on holding grudges and staying angry. These emotions are part of our past where the ego is most comfortable. But it also occurred to me that in order to live in the Now, I had to recognize the fact that if I had not lived all the moments of my life, I would not be at this time and place. In other words, every experience I've had, and every person I've met on this journey called life has played a role in who I am and where I am physically, emotionally and spiritually.

Next, I reflected on the second tenet, *Forgiveness of Others,* and the challenges we face overcoming our negative feelings, emotions and experiences towards those people who have hurt us. It occurred to me that each day we encounter—directly and indirectly—people we don't particularly like as well as situations that contribute to our negative mindset and insecurity. I'm referring not only to negative news and the horrible deeds perpetrated by rogue governments and dictators, but also the suffering and heartaches of those people we know and love.

As I used my shillelagh to sweep away the broken twigs that littered the cart path, I recalled meeting a quiet, but competent, accountant named John who worked for a non-profit organization in Los Angeles that had retained me as a leadership coach. It was obvious to me that John was under-employed given his talent and experience in finance. One day, we had lunch and I asked him why he worked as an under-paid accountant for this particular organization that helped find temporary shelter for displaced families. This was the story he told me.

John revealed to me he was an alcoholic. He had lost his high-paying job at a prestigious CPA firm and his family abandoned him due to his excessive drinking and abusive behavior. According to John, he put his family through "a living hell" for seven years before he finally joined Alcoholics Anonymous and completed its Twelve Steps program. That was almost four years ago.

Today, John is proud to call himself a recovering alcoholic. He has a meaningful job with the non-profit organization and he volunteers twice a week at AA meetings to help others overcome their disease and addiction to alcohol and drugs. He proudly told me he had been sober for more than two years.

Sadly, John's wife and two teenage children left him and moved to Minneapolis. John understood why they left given his abusive nature and battle with alcoholism. Still, John tried to maintain contact by sending letters and cards to his family on their birthdays and other special occasions. But they chose not to communicate with him for several years. Then, four months ago, John said he met his daughter for the first time in nearly seven years. For some reason, she reached out to her father. For John, their brief meeting was a moment of great joy, but also, agonizing pain.

When John saw his daughter he realized so much had changed. He hardly recognized her. She was now 24 and had graduated from college. She had a full-time job as a hotel sales manager in St. Paul. During their 30 minutes together at a local Starbucks in Los Angeles, John asked her forgiveness for all he had done to hurt her and destroy their family. He apologized for denying her a father during a very important time in her life.

John told me he did not want to cry, but tears welled up in his eyes when she said, "But Dad, you missed my high school and college graduations. You weren't there for our father-daughter dances. I had no one to talk to about Economics and English Literature. You never knew about my high school senior class trip to Washington, D.C., and you never visited me at my college. Your own son didn't invite you to his wedding four years ago because he couldn't trust you to not get drunk and ruin the most important day of his life. And did you know you have two grandsons?"

John told me he could feel his heart breaking as his daughter spoke each word. He knew nothing about his son's marriage or the birth of his two grandsons. Emotionally, John was stunned. His daughter's words and images cut into him so deeply that he wanted to crawl into a hole and die. John knew he had broken his daughter's heart; and after she left, he sobbed for two days. It was a gut-wrenching experience for him, but he resolved to never again do anything that would hurt his family or himself. He remained sober throughout this painful period.

John also made up his mind to continue his subtle efforts to reach out to his wife and son in the hopes that one day, if the opportunity presented itself, he could ask their forgiveness for all the pain and misery he had caused them. He told me that before his daughter left, he asked her to do one thing—to let his son and wife know that, "I've changed. I've been sober for two years and I'm different now. Please tell them I am very sorry for the pain and suffering I caused all of you. I hope you will forgive me."

While their meeting ended cordially, there were no hugs or goodbye kisses. John knew he had hurt his daughter. It was a pain he would never forget as his daughter politely ended the conversation by looking at her watch, then excused herself and left by taxi for the airport, leaving behind the searing images of a negligent father who had squandered the love of his family and missed the best days of his life—and, for what? Although he has not heard from his daughter since their meeting in Los Angeles, John told me he remains optimistic. He is confident that one day he will be reunited with his family.

While I was hopeful for John, I knew that seven years was a long time for a husband and wife to be estranged. People change and move on. They start anew. I feared that perhaps his daughter knew more than she revealed to her father at that meeting. But I said nothing to him because hope is a powerful force in people's lives and can sustain them and their love forever.

Before we ended our lunch, John told me as part of his volunteer work, he counsels other alcoholics on the emotional price they will pay. John tells them his story. He reminds them, "If you don't change your ways, you'll suffer the same loneliness and isolation I've suffered. It isn't worth it. Be very careful of your choices in life because you reap what you sow."

As I looped around the back of Mt. Woodson Golf Course's 13th hole that connected two par 5s, I thought about forgiveness and people like John. I realized that his ability to forgive himself and seek the forgiveness of those he loved so deeply, but hurt so bad, were hallmarks of the Second Sacred Question. I also concluded that faith in self and a relationship with the Divine Source is part of the forgiveness equation.

This is how people like John overcome the heartaches and pain that haunt them once they have recovered from their self-destructive habits and abusive lifestyle. While I knew it would probably take a miracle for John's family to forgive him and allow him back in their lives, I could see John had taken the necessary steps to rebuild his life and create a life worth living. As he told me, "In my most desperate hour, I came to the realization that I would either die from alcohol or change. I had to accept the fact that we all have a past. You've now heard mine. I know it's both unpleasant and in many respects despicable. What you haven't heard is my tomorrows—and this is what keeps me alive now—the chance to make today right and the hope that tomorrow will be even better."

I was tiring a bit as I approached the long, steep hill that leads to the elevated 17th tee box with its spectacular view of Mt. Woodson and the Ramona Valley to the northeast. John's story stayed in my mind. One of the lessons *The Course of 10,000 Days*® teaches us is that for every action, there is a reaction; and for every reaction, there can be a thoughtful response. That response should be one of compassion, forgiveness and love whenever possible. If we do not give, we cannot receive. If we do not love, we will not be loved in return. If we do not forgive, we will not be forgiven. If we are not kind and merciful to others, the world will make each day a time of toil and hardship for us.

It is difficult work to change our beliefs, values, behaviors and attitudes. We easily get set in our ways. We grow comfortable with our routines, habits, grudges, animosity and negative thoughts. In fact, we become so comfortable living in our velvet rut that we don't want to climb out of it. But if we want to find our higher purpose, we must challenge the way we currently see things and take the necessary steps to improve our lives. This is how our Inner Spirit can help us and guide us to a better life. I was convinced that John was sincere and contrite. While forgiveness could never undo the damage and pain he caused his family, at least he had taken the necessary steps to climb out of his rut and get his life back on track. I told him so as we left the restaurant that day and I thanked him for sharing his story of forgiveness, courage and recovery with me.

By practicing the virtues of compassion, forgiveness and kindness, we learn *how* to love all persons and living things. We learn how to be merciful towards those who have offended us. Most importantly, we learn how to discover our divineness. Love and forgiveness are the cornerstones of human divineness and the key to entering the Kingdom of Roses.

The Course reminds us that while each of us has imperfections, we are, for the most part, decent, loving human beings. *The Course* encourages us to embrace all people in an effort to help us overturn our Four Stones. And *The Course* especially encourages us to take the first step—the most difficult step—to extend our hands and hearts to those who have asked us for forgiveness and want to make amends for their mistakes. This is at the core of what the second tenet of the Second Sacred Question teaches.

As I reached the 17th tee box, the sun had warmed the autumn air and I stopped to drink a cup of water. I removed my baseball cap to wipe the sweat from my brow. I looked at the logo on my cap that read, "Kick it up a notch." I smiled to myself because forgiveness was also about *kicking it up a notch*. In other words, if we are not willing to change our ways, we remain the same. We atrophy and eventually, we die unfulfilled and unhappy. Life is about change and trying to improve ourselves and the world we live in. Forgiveness is part of that change process. True transformation cannot happen until we have addressed the forgiveness question. This was on my mind as I contemplated the third tenet of the Second Sacred Question, *What are you doing today to take ownership of your life?*

I realized that John had begun to take ownership of his life. When I heard John's story about his battle with alcoholism and how he hurt the people he loved most, I realized there are risks in everything we do. In many ways, life is a balancing act in which we have to filter out the negative messages and replace them with positive thoughts. Over a lifetime, our ego registers every comment, opinion, remark, glance and implication directed at us by every person we have ever met or encountered. Typically, our ego gives more credence to the negative messages than the positive ones to shield us from danger and keep us from venturing outside our comfort zone. In other words, our ego does not like us to take risks! In John's case, he risked facing a new reality by getting sober. As an alcoholic, the full impact of his self-destructive behavior was dulled by his constant state of drunkenness. As a recovering alcoholic, he could clearly comprehend the destruction he had caused as well as the pain he had inflicted on his family. I wondered to myself, "How does someone begin to forgive themselves under such circumstances?"

This question reminded me of the work of Dr. Fred Luskin, the Co-Director of the Stanford-Northern Ireland HOPE Project, who said, "Forgiveness is a gift we give ourselves for our own wellness to free us from the past in order to move forward." Perhaps, people like John understood this better than those of us who have never experienced such self-destruction.

The Course teaches us a powerful prayer by Swami Sivananda. It is entitled the *Prayer of Forgiveness*:

If anyone speaks ill of you, praise him always.
If anyone injures you, serve him nicely.
If anyone persecutes you, help him in all possible ways.
You will attain immense strength
You will control anger and pride.
You will enjoy peace, poise and serenity.
You will become Divine.

The Course also reminds us that we have suppressed memories of negative things that happened in our life that we would rather forget— things we do not want to talk about or be reminded of. But this is why we have a conscience—to keep us from repeating the same mistakes and to help us become more tolerant and compassionate.

The Course teaches us that one way people can sustain love is to have compassion and perform good deeds for others. *The Course* also reminds us that Forgiveness is an act of compassion and ultimately, an act of love. It is also an effective antidote to anger and stress. We should never doubt our basic goodness because we are born with a heart that knows only love and a powerful Inner Spirit that knows only goodness. Robert A. Johnson expressed it this way when he said, "The challenge of life is for each of us to find our profound nobility of character."

As I studied the Second Sacred Question, it occurred to me that this was a time to examine my life without letting my ego suppress negative memories or justify past actions that made me uncomfortable. I began to understand that the Second Sacred Question is not really about my past, but rather, the present and how I treat others and myself. It is about who I am now and where I am going in life. It is also about how I will get there. I began to understand how *The Course* interpreted Forgiveness.

Until we forgive others and seek their forgiveness, we will remain emotionally stuck in that uncomfortable place and time. Forgiveness is the key to moving on and creating a life of purpose, peace and passion. Forgiveness is also the key to unlocking the door to our Inner Spirit. By dealing directly with Forgiveness I was quieting my ego. I also was allowing my Inner Spirit to surface. It was a cathartic moment for me.

Buddha addressed people by referring to them as "O Nobly Born." This was Buddha's way of validating human beings. He believed all persons were nobly born. He believed all people were inherently good. He understood that most human beings allow their egos to control their thoughts which, in turn, corrupts their actions and causes them to make mistakes and offend others. That is part of life's learning experience. We all make mistakes. It's not a perfect world. So, just move on, but learn the lesson—how not to repeat those same mistakes.

The Course also teaches us that Forgiveness and Compassion should never be confused for weakness. They are signs of strength because it takes courage to forgive someone and have compassion towards another person, especially when they do not like you.

This brought to mind one of the most touching stories I had ever heard on the speaking circuit about Forgiveness and Compassion. It dealt with a single mother in Detroit who raised her teenage son to be a good boy. He did his homework, worked hard at his part-time job, respected his elders, avoided trouble and followed his mother's rules. One night, her son was shot and killed during an armed robbery as he worked behind the counter of a convenience store located only four blocks from his home. The shooter was a 15-year-old gang member. When the young employee recognized the robbers from his neighborhood they shot him. Eventually, the shooter was apprehended and convicted of murder. The victim's mother was angry, hurt and bent on revenge. At the young murderer's sentencing, she stood up, glared at him and with hateful eyes cried out, "I'm going to kill you!"

Several months after the trial, the distraught mother decided that she would go to the juvenile detention center and visit this despicable hoodlum who had taken her son's life. She told herself it was her duty to remind the young thug what a horrible person he was for taking the life of her only child. Over the next few years, she frequently made the 30-minute trip by bus to the detention center to talk with the young criminal about his actions and show him pictures of her son so he would never forget what he had done. But as time passed, the bereaved mother took on a different attitude. She began to ask the young man about his childhood, parents, family and goals knowing someday he would leave prison and have a second chance at life, unlike her dead son.

For two years, she regularly visited the young convict. One day, the young man told her, "Ma'am, for two years you've come here to visit me. I know you hate me for what I did, and you even said at my trial that you wanted to kill me. And there isn't a day that goes by when I don't think about your son and regret what I did. It was senseless and something I must live with for the rest of my life. But most of all, when I see you here and you bring me things to help me get by, well, I'm sorry for what I did. I'm sorry I hurt you. I hope someday you will forgive me."

Hearing the words of the repentant criminal, the mother said nothing. She quietly got up from the visitors' room and left. She never returned to see the prisoner again. But when the convicted man turned 18, he had his first parole hearing. Seated in the hearing room was the victim's mother. The convict knew he stood no chance of making parole if the mother spoke against him. When the parole board asked the mother if she wanted to address the board, she softly replied, "Yes."

She stood up and told the parole board, "For two years after this young man was imprisoned for murdering my son, I often came here to visit him. I was angry, bitter and hated him for taking my only child and devastating my life. He took from me everything I loved including my reason for living. When I last came to the prison, this young man found it in his heart to ask for my forgiveness. I could not forgive him then. But now, I realize that we all make mistakes. My mistake was holding on to my bitterness and not opening my heart to his plea for forgiveness.

"In forgiving him, I know that I will never be able to bury my pain and suffering. I cannot forget what happened or what this young man took from me. But now, I am asking this parole board to give this young man another chance at life. I am asking you to grant his parole and allow him to come live with me. If you do that, I will give him the home he never had, the mother he never knew and the love he never experienced as a child. If he will agree to live in my home, and you will allow me to help him get back on his feet and make a success of his life, I will accept him as my own."

Stunned by her compassion and forgiveness, the young convict covered his face and wept openly. The mother approached him, and for the first time, they embraced. She had shown compassion and forgiveness. He was granted parole and lived with the woman for five years as he earned his high school and college degrees. When he graduated, he secured a good-paying job as a software engineer. Today, 10 years after the mother adopted her son's murderer, the young man is married and has two sons. Now, the mother who had lost her reason for living when her own son was murdered, has a new family to care for and shower with love. And while there will always be the pain of loss, the mother has found a way to use forgiveness and compassion to overcome her loss and fill her cup with goodness and love.

As I reflected on this story of the mother and the repentant convict, I knew the mother—despite her pain and loss—had been able to find love through forgiveness. She had to embrace forgiveness in order to heal herself. As *The Course* teaches us, the past is past. When you forgive, you must also give up all hope of finding a better past because there is none.

Every day there are random acts of kindness and forgiveness we can perform that help us achieve a higher level of peace and satisfaction. I am referring to the small things we do that often go unnoticed except for the people who benefit from our kindness. For example, giving up my seat on the crowded rental car shuttle bus to a woman who was carrying a child in one arm and a suitcase in another; forgiving the student on the airplane who whacked me with her backpack as she made her way down the narrow aisle; allowing the driver in front of me to change lanes at the last moment to exit the freeway and not honking my horn at him for failing to use his turn signal.

My list could go on, but I have made my point. Every day, as Mother Teresa noted, we have numerous opportunities to do many small things with great kindness and forgiveness. It occurred to me that when I allow my Inner Spirit to guide my thoughts and actions, life's situations often take a turn for the better.

Forgiveness of Self requires us to have compassion for ourselves and others because we cannot love as long as our heart is filled with resentment, anger or hatred. Compassion requires us to forgive those who offend us so we can return to a state of love. Compassion also allows us to accept responsibility for who we are and change those things that keep us from achieving our higher purpose.

Forgiveness is a two-step process with each step supporting the other. First, you must forgive yourself. Secondly, before you can take ownership of your life, you must forgive others so all the hurdles for future success are cleared.

This is why *The Course* challenges us to forgive ourselves for all the dumb things we have done. Without compassion, forgiveness is impossible. The reason forgiveness is so difficult is that only our Inner Spirit can initiate the process. Our ego is incapable of forgiveness because the ego interprets forgiveness as a sign of weakness.

This explains why our ego thrives on turmoil and discord. It also explains why revenge and anger are such destructive emotions. They fuel the fires of our ego. As long as we are defensive, the ego remains in control. As long as we are judgmental, the ego is in control. As long as our heart is bitter, the ego is still in control. Regrettably, the ego alone cannot lead us to our higher purpose, peace or happiness. It also requires the guidance and participation of our Inner Spirit. And only through Forgiveness of Self is our higher purpose revealed to us.

As I completed my morning walk along the freshly watered 18th fairway, I reflected on the second tenet, Forgiveness of Others, and the writings of Dr. Kavi in his book *The Course of 10,000 Days®' Path to Forgiveness*. This short work is handwritten and contains Kavi's personal thoughts and writings on the subject of Forgiveness as well as quotes from persons he respects. This little book provided me with great insights on the three tenets of the Second Sacred Question.

Dr. Kavi wrote, "The subject of Forgiveness is powerful, but very complex. For some people, Forgiveness is about letting go. For others, it's about forgiving, but *not* forgetting. For some, Forgiveness is a matter of reconciliation or reparation."

Another passage dealt with Dr. Kavi's thoughts on the question of whether Forgiveness also requires one to *forget* the incident that caused the pain in the first place. He quotes Rabbi Harold Kushner who said, "The central question is *not* whether someone should forgive, but rather *how* to forgive without forgetting." According to Rabbi Kushner, "Forgiveness happens inside us and represents letting go of the role of victim."

In another passage, Dr. Kavi quotes South African Archbishop Desmond Tutu, the 1984 Nobel Peace Prize recipient, who said, "Without memory, there can be no healing; and without Forgiveness, there can be no future."

As I turned and headed home, I reflected on both quotes knowing they came from men who understand the importance of Forgiveness. Rabbi Kushner knew from members of his synagogue about the persecution of Jews during World War II under the Nazis. Archbishop Tutu experienced the brutality of Apartheid, a system of racial segregation that was enforced in South Africa from 1948 to 1994 to ensure that South Africans of European descent maintained their economic and political dominance. Fortunately, significant changes have occurred in Germany and South Africa. Both nations have become role models for healing a nation's soul and each has found success and prosperity through Forgiveness.

In a talk on Forgiveness, Archbishop Tutu said, "To forgive is not just to be altruistic. It is the best form of self-interest. It is also a process that does not exclude hatred or anger. These emotions are all part of being human. You should never hate yourself for hating others who do terrible things because the depth of your love is shown by the extent of your anger."

Dr. Kavi's book also contains several references to the power of forgiveness. He quotes two British writers, Dr. Thomas Fuller and Lord Edward Herbert who were credited with saying, "He that cannot forgive others breaks the bridge over which he himself must pass if he would reach heaven; for everyone has need to be forgiven."

Kavi also quotes Horace Bushnell who said, "Forgiveness is man's deepest need and highest achievement." I reflected on these quotes for a few minutes as the fog thickened above the trees surrounding the lush green fairways. A few instances came to mind where I was upset or angry with someone because they had either deceived me or mistreated me. Had I forgiven them? If not, did I burn the bridge I needed to cross over so I could discover my higher purpose? I realized that Fuller's and Herbert's quote had both relevance and meaning for me. I also thought about Bushnell's definition of Forgiveness as man's "highest achievement." It was hard to argue with Bushnell's interpretation knowing that until I could forgive myself and others for past wrongs, I would never be able to discover my higher purpose.

CHAPTER 17

Emotional Mapping

Over a lifetime, our ego helps to shape our personality. It is a composite based on all of our experiences, relationships, comments and opinions others have of us as well as our own emotions and feelings. As we grow from a child to an adult, our character and personality develop memory patterns based on our life experiences. *The Course* refers to this process as *Emotional Mapping*. Through the process of *Emotional Mapping*, we can trace the development of our unique personality as well as how and why we responded to certain events and significant situations that impacted our life. For example, situations like how and where we were raised, our relationships with family and friends, religious influences and schooling—all these factors have an impact on who we are and how we respond to the challenges we face in life.

But there are also more subtle situations that often go undetected that affect our emotional map. For example, did we have friends in school or were we deemed different because we wore glasses, had braces or got straight A's? Did we have a date for our high school prom or not attend because we didn't know how to dance? Did we pass our driver's license test on the first attempt? Did we gain admission to a respectable college?

These critical events shape and impact us. They can boost our confidence or lower our self-esteem. And their accumulated effect on us can have significant consequences as we get older because our memory never forgets how we felt and how we responded.

The more negative the messages, experiences and memories we've internalized, the more damaged we are—mentally and emotionally. To undo the damage, we seek various types of treatments and cures—medical, psychological and spiritual. The longer our negative *Emotional Mapping* goes untreated, the more problems it can cause to our mental, physical and spiritual dimensions.

During the first half of our Discovery Years, from birth until the age of 14, our unique personality is formed and set. For the most part, we accept this *Emotional Mapping* process without question because we don't know how to challenge it or refute it. For example, our name, birth parents, relatives, nationality, race, religion, appearance and language are pre-mapped elements of our personality. This includes decisions made for us by our biological parents or adopted parents. From birth, our ego internalizes these characteristics and experiences to form our unique emotional map. Who we are is a complex matter, but we must also know who we are *not*. This is why *The Course of 10,000 Days®* is an invaluable tool for helping us confront certain assumptions, lies and negative opinions we internalized at a young age and came to believe about ourselves despite the fact they might not be true—or, at least, incomplete or inaccurate.

Regrettably, most people live their lives without ever challenging certain teachings, assumptions and opinions they learned in their Discovery Years. Instead, they blindly accept erroneous data and negative information about themselves as fact. This includes vitriolic words from parents and others we admire that are delivered in a hurtful and destructive manner. The comments and opinions spoken by family, relatives, friends and teachers have the most profound impact on us—for better or worse. Sometimes we hurt those we love the most. The degree of each person's self-worth and self-love are contingent upon how their ego interprets those statements, assumptions and opinions made by others.

If, for example, a parent withholds love from a child, or offers only conditional love based on a child's acceptable behavior or performance, that type of psychological and emotional mistreatment may have devastating consequences on the child's social and emotional development. On the other hand, if a child is raised in a nurturing, loving environment where he or she receives positive reinforcement and praise, then that child's *Emotional Map* will include a higher level of self-esteem and a stronger sense of self-awareness and inner security.

The Course of 10,000 Days® offers us a way to exorcize the hell from our lives by challenging false assumptions and creating a new *Emotional Map*—one that is based on who we *really* are. But this process requires us to challenge those misleading statements, lies and false opinions and replace them with new belief statements that accurately reflect who we are *now*.

Too many people grow up believing they are not worthy to achieve success or live their dreams because of the hurtful, thoughtless statements made by someone they loved or trusted whether intended or not. However, we can undo those negative feelings of self-doubt and inferiority and create a healthy self-image. It is important to remember that we are not the same person today as that five-year-old, 15-year-old or 30-year-old we see in family photographs. We've changed. We've matured. Our physical and emotional states are different today than they were 25 years ago. So, we need to let go of those negative emotional weights that bind us to the past and adopt a new perspective that is based on a healthy appraisal of our talents and skills that will put us on track with our vision and higher purpose.

This is why forgiveness begins by forgiving yourself. In order to forgive yourself, you must acknowledge two crucial concepts: First, you are a perfect being in the eyes of the Divine Source. That does not mean that every golf shot you hit will be perfect or every task you undertake will be successful. But it does mean you are endowed with the gifts and attributes necessary to achieve human divineness on earth. Second, you will never be fulfilled as long as you try to live your life according to the expectations and opinions of others.

The Course teaches that to break free from the chains of negative *Emotional Mapping* you must have compassion for yourself. You must believe you are complete in the eyes of the Divine Source and worthy of being loved as well as capable of loving others. It all starts with acceptance and forgiveness.

CHAPTER 18

Acceptance

*T*he *Course* also helped me learn to accept myself. I learned how to overcome my vulnerabilities in responding truthfully to the Three Sacred Questions. My greatest challenge was getting past my ego because I knew my ego would resist my attempts to probe deeply for meaningful answers.

But being vulnerable is an expression of our humanness. *The Course* teaches us that in order to resurrect our Inner Spirit, we must be honest with ourselves and not be embarrassed or afraid to admit our shortcomings and mistakes. We all make mistakes and experience failure from time to time. This is a natural part of life; and, it also marks the Acceptance of Self phase of *The Course*.

In most recovery programs, this step is commonly referred to as surrendering. Yet, too often, our ego confuses surrender with defeat. Ironically, just the opposite is true. *The Course* teaches us that the process of surrender—or letting go of those thoughts, behaviors, emotions and actions that hold us back in life—is actually victory over the ego's domination because it allows our Inner Spirit to surface and guide us to our higher purpose.

Surrender is merely acknowledging that our past behavior and practices were either destructive or leading us in the wrong direction. Thus, surrender is merely accepting what is—for better or for worse. As Dr. Kavi reminded me, "Facts are friendly, sometimes harsh, but always fair." Nevertheless, our ego wants us to think otherwise. According to our ego, surrender is losing control. It is giving up.

In order to confront this serious issue that will block us from crossing over the Bridge of Forgiveness and moving on with our life, *The Course* recommends an exercise in which we ask ourselves two difficult questions:

Are you living a life of truth or a lie? Validate your answer.

If you are living a lie, do you want to spend your whole life deceiving yourself and others, or do you want to live a life of truth through which purpose, peace and passion can be attained?

If you are living a life of truth, you will know it because you can validate and measure your actions against those values and beliefs that transcend culture and time. If you cannot justify your life by measuring it against the values and standards that you know to be truthful, you are living a lie.

Armed with this knowledge, you must ask yourself the second question. If your answer is "No, I do not want to spend my whole life living a lie," then you must make the decision to change your thoughts, behaviors and actions.

Sometimes change is very difficult because we believe so strongly in something. As Saint Thomas Aquinas counseled in his famous writing, *Summa Theologica*, "A thing is known according to the knower." In other words, we each have our own interpretation of what is the truth and how things should be in life. However, simply having an opinion about something or espousing a particular belief does not make you right. There could be another answer—a different response that is based on the truth instead of opinions, misinformation, prophecy and hearsay.

This is one reason why fundamentalist thinking is flawed. This applies to religion as well as science, politics and all disciplines in which dogmatists do the thinking for the masses. So much of what fundamentalists believe is rooted in mythology, anecdotal accounts and misinformation that have been interpreted to have but one meaning—theirs—rather than multiple interpretations. This practice of limited thinking is merely an excuse to perpetuate self-righteousness and breed ignorance. It is also a clear sign that the ego is in control rather than a testament of one's wisdom and enlightenment.

Returning to the importance of surrender and acceptance, it's not uncommon for most people who are confronting their demons to go through the seven stages of grief or some variation thereof. Those seven stages are shock, denial, bargaining, guilt, anger, depression and hope or acceptance. This is all part of the surrendering process in which we come to terms with wanting to live a life worth remembering.

Perhaps this is what St. Paul was trying to teach us in his writings about Jesus' dual role as both a mortal man and a divine being. St. Paul, who was the architect of Christianity, believed that Jesus' resurrection was not merely one of surrendering his flesh and bones, but also a transformation—the resurrection of his Inner Spirit which explains how Jesus could be both human and divine. As a mortal man, Jesus was vulnerable to many of the same struggles between his ego and Inner Spirit that you and I are subject to.

This is noted throughout the New Testament. Jesus was tempted by the devil. He got angry at the moneychangers in the temple. He admonished Peter for cutting off the ear of the guard who arrested him in the Garden of Gethsemane. He bargained with God while dying on the cross and eventually, came to accept his fate as a man.

Unlike other men, Jesus at this stage in his life had learned how to lead with his heart instead of his ego. His guiding principles were love, compassion and forgiveness. By the time Jesus began his ministry, he had mastered many of the same principles that are taught in *The Course*. Jesus had transcended his ego and this allowed him to live through his Inner Spirit and ultimately, connect with his divineness.

Throughout the gospels are poignant stories of Jesus' humanness. The human struggles that Jesus faced in terms of balancing his ego and his Inner Spirit are no different from the struggles you and I face today. Like us, Jesus had to make the transition from being ego driven to allow his Inner Spirit to guide him to achieve his higher purpose and divineness.

Every person must find their own way in allowing their Inner Spirit to surface. Some people meditate to calm their ego. Others control their ego through prayer or in service to others. Some retreat to a monastic life and dedicate themselves to serving others. You can find various ways to help your Inner Spirit surface. Some people practice spiritual renewal exercises such as yoga or Tai Chi. These disciplines help us attain a state of spiritual insight and tranquility by accessing our Inner Spirit.

Despite all these tools, exercises and disciplines, few people in their Discovery Years and Fulfillment Years identify their higher purpose. We're too busy earning a paycheck, raising children, trying to get a promotion at work or saving enough money to buy a house. But, as the years go by, our Inner Spirit starts to gnaw away by posing questions that make us wonder what we're doing with our life and how we'll live a life worth remembering. My experience has been that most people begin to awaken to a spiritual calling sometime during their 40s or 50s. That's when our Legacy Years begin for most of us.

Our Inner Spirit knows that with few exceptions we are traveling through life as pretenders. We are play-actors because we are not utilizing the talents we have been given by the Divine Source. We're just showing up and doing what is expected of us. Our ego disguises itself behind a mask of doing what is socially acceptable in order to fool us into thinking we are making a difference with our lives. But, it's just a tactic on the ego's part to stay in control.

Given the opportunity, our Inner Spirit would rise up and challenge us to live a life worth remembering. Understand your ego is a master at deceit and deception. It's very good at suffocating the voice of your Inner Spirit and staying in control. We've unwittingly allowed our ego to enjoy years of practice at controlling our life at the expense of our Inner Spirit!

Breaking the grip of the ego is a major challenge during our 20s and 30s because we are busy living our Discovery Years and Fulfillment Years. These are exciting times! We're making major decisions that affect our future; and, many of these decisions are made without the benefit of our Inner Spirit because it remains suppressed. While our Inner Spirit is conscious and aware of our needs, it only surfaces intermittently because we are so consumed with matters of the ego.

I'm talking about decisions such as: Where should I attend school? Where should I live after college? What job should I accept? Which social events should I attend? Whom should I date? Whom should I marry? Should we have children? Which neighborhood should we live in? Should we buy a house or rent? And so forth. During our first 10,000 days and well into our Fulfillment Years, we make decisions that chart our course in life. It is only when we have mastered our job or raised our children that we can focus our thoughts on the task of finding our higher purpose. It is at this point we begin to hear the quiet voice of our Inner Spirit trying to reach us. For most people, this happens in their mid-40s or early 50s.

It takes this long because cultivating our Inner Spirit requires maturity and we mature at different times and stages. Life is a journey and each person travels his or her own unique path. In fact, no two journeys are the same. I could be your identical twin and we would arrive at different places at the end of our journeys. So, connecting with your Inner Spirit, developing a trust bond with your Inner Spirit and allowing it to guide you, requires you to be at the right place at the right time—mentally, spiritually and emotionally—in order for everything to click. Certainly, maturity is a key factor in terms of being receptive to your Inner Spirit's overtures, and that is one reason why these questions rarely surface until we approach or reach our Legacy Years.

CHAPTER 19

The Vancouver Conversation

In October, I traveled to Vancouver where Ajay and I were invited to speak at the Pacific Rim Leadership Conference. The October afternoon air was unseasonably warm as I arrived in Vancouver. The sun shone on the incredible snow-capped mountains in the distance. The Strait of Georgia, which drains into the northern Pacific Ocean, sparkled with its crystal blue colors. Vancouver has a cosmopolitan flair that makes it one of the most dynamic and beautiful cities in North America.

The conference schedule was fast-paced and kept us busy for two days with our presentations, social events and a harbor cruise. Finally, on the third day after the closing session ended at 11:00 am, Ajay and I left the Four Seasons Vancouver Hotel and drove through Stanley Park and across the Lions Gate Bridge to Horseshoe Bay, a picturesque community located 40 minutes northwest of downtown Vancouver. There, we sat on the outdoor deck at Sewell's Marina drinking a cold beer while watching the tourists and locals come and go. It was a good place to continue our discussion on the subject of Forgiveness.

Ajay shared with me some passages from Dr. Kavi's book. The first quote was by Archbishop Desmond Tutu who said, "True forgiveness deals with the past, all the past, to make the future possible. We cannot go on nursing grudges even vicariously for those who cannot speak for themselves any longer. We have to accept that we do what we do for generations past, present and yet to come. That is what makes a community a community or a people a people—for better or for worse."

The second quote Ajay cited from Kavi's book came from Marianne Williamson's *Illuminata*. She writes, "The choice to follow love through to its completion is the choice to seek completion within ourselves. The point at which we shut down on others is the point at which we shut down on life. We heal as we heal others, and we heal others by extending our perceptions past their weaknesses. Until we have seen someone's darkness, we don't really know who that person is. Until we have forgiven someone's darkness, we don't really know what love is. Forgiving others is the only way to forgive ourselves, and forgiveness is our greatest need."

"Forgiveness is much more than an emotion," Ajay told me. "I believe Forgiveness is the single greatest barrier to peace, both personally and in terms of stability in our world." Mahatma Gandhi said, "The weak can never forgive. Forgiveness is the attribute of the strong." This is why the process of Forgiveness begins with yourself. This is why the first tenet of the Second Sacred Question is *Have you forgiven yourself for past mistakes and wrongdoings?*

Ajay shared one final quote from Dr. Kavi's book that helped me appreciate the importance of forgiving myself. It was from Carolyn Myss' book, *Anatomy of the Spirit*. She writes, "When we harbor negative emotions towards others or toward ourselves; or, when we intentionally create pain for others, we poison our own physical and spiritual systems. By far, the strongest poison to the human spirit is the inability to forgive oneself or another person. It disables a person's emotional resources."

Harboring negative emotions is harmful to your physical and emotional well-being. If you are not aware of your negative emotions, you need to be. Once you become aware, then you must take action to eliminate those negative practices. This is the essence of Forgiveness.

Ironically, most people don't think Forgiveness applies to them. Their ego constantly says, "You've done nothing wrong. You don't need to apologize for anything! You are right and they are wrong."

Our ego thrives on being right at the expense of our fulfillment. But, of course, the ego tells us these things so it can remain in control. The issue of Forgiveness pits your Inner Spirit squarely against the powerful forces of your ego. This is why Forgiveness of yourself is essential to getting past certain barriers and moving on with your life.

The Course teaches us that the Negative Three R's—Resistance, Resentment and Revenge—are the primary reason we have difficulty seeking or granting forgiveness. When your heart is consumed with one or more of the Negative Three R's it doesn't take much to activate your negative emotions.

Of course, you are your ego. So, you have to accept responsibility for what you say and how you react and respond. Ironically, this is the ego's ultimate betrayal of self because revenge accomplishes nothing except to complicate life and harm others. Crimes of passion happen because the ego is hell bent on revenge. Your ego is not interested in healing or seeking help to alleviate the stress and pressures of life. Only the Inner Spirit can achieve this outcome. This is why it's so difficult for people to seriously address Forgiveness and its three tenets when their ego is in control and unleashes such weapons as the Negative Three R's to assert its presence.

In everyday life we encounter people, things and situations that we would rather not deal with. Again, when you consider the fact that our ego resists most change, it's understandable why we perceive certain people and situations as a threat rather than an opportunity. For these reasons, we oftentimes resist opportunities that can move us forward.

It's only natural for someone to resist forgiving another person for hurtful words or actions. Louise Hay said, "Resistance is the first step to change." When we begin to feel our feelings, it is the start of a healthy process that can ultimately lead to Forgiveness.

In his book, Dr. Kavi writes, "Forgiveness is the second greatest sacrifice any person can make because it requires a person to overcome their bitterness and anger which is buried deep within their heart and seek out their Inner Spirit for guidance and direction. Only at this stage can Forgiveness be achieved."

Within every person a battle is waged between good and evil. As the fifth century Roman Christian poet Aurelius Clemens Prudentius suggested in his epic poem *Psychomachia* (or *Contest of the Soul*), we must constantly choose between virtue and vice. And while many times we succumb to the vices, which Prudentius dubbed *the seven deadly sins*, I believe there are many more acts of humility, kindness and forgiveness taking place each day than there are acts of wrath, gluttony, lust, greed, sloth, envy and pride. Helen Keller said, "Although the world is full of suffering, it is also full of the overcoming of it."

Of course, we must look for it! Unfortunately, people are conditioned through their egos to expect bad news instead of the silver lining in clouds. I suppose this is why newspapers and the evening news broadcasts lead with misery, death, war, floods and famine. We anticipate bad news, yet good things are also happening all around us.

Peace does not happen randomly. It requires only one person who has the courage and vision to humbly step forward and lead the masses down a better path. Perhaps the most memorable symbol of peace are the photos of that one brave, unknown protester—dubbed The Tank Man— who stood down Chinese tanks as they rolled into the middle of Beijing's Tiananmen Square on June 4, 1989 to squash a national protest. He stood there alone and faced down the tanks which could have easily killed him. His courage proved how weak and vulnerable the Chinese Communist leadership was at that time and forced significant changes and reform in how China governs today.

Perhaps the problem with warring nations is a lack of visionary leadership. Enlightened leaders choose peace over war. *The Course* tells us that when countries resort to war and violence, their national egos are in control, not their Inner Spirit.

Sometimes the masses are unwilling to embrace the message of peace and the messenger is slain. Jesus, Gandhi and Martin Luther King, Jr. suffered this unkind fate. However, once the peace quest has started it cannot be stopped. Such is the power of good and forgiveness. Eventually, people will realize that the journey towards peace is worth making because it offers us hope for a better tomorrow.

Our ego has a difficult time coming to terms with admitting fault and seeking forgiveness from others for past wrongs we have committed. It's contrary to the ego's core constitution. This is why *The Course* asks us to seek forgiveness from others. It is a conscious decision we make to suppress our ego and allow our Inner Spirit's voice to be heard. In seeking the forgiveness of others—whether directly by asking their forgiveness, or indirectly, by confessing our wrongs or praying to the Divine Source for forgiveness—we cleanse our soul and our conscience. And also, we humble ourselves in the eyes of the Divine Source. Through humility, we are able to see our mistakes, make amends and resolve to live a better life.

In Dr. Kavi's book, he cites an Islamic prayer that *The Course* invites us to offer whenever we need to humble ourselves and seek forgiveness. It reads:

> *O God, forgive me my delinquency and ignorance; my immoderation in my concerns, and also that fault of mine whereof Thou are better aware than myself. O God, forgive me my earnestness and my sport, my error and my design. All these failings are in me. O God, forgive me for that which I hasten and for that which I defer, for that which I conceal*

and for that which I reveal; also for that fault of mine whereof Thou art better aware than myself. Thou art the Deferrer, and over all things, Thou art Omnipotent.

Sophocles said, "The prayer of one pure heart has the power to atone for many." What *The Course* teaches us with regard to the second tenet is that when we seek forgiveness, we open our heart to love. The expression of sorrow is the first step to Forgiveness. The ego will fight you on this, but you must allow your Inner Spirit to guide you through this challenging process. By reaching out to those we have offended, we are asking their forgiveness for our actions. Through forgiveness, we cleanse our hearts and allow grace to fill our soul.

The act of Forgiveness is really a transformational process. *The Course* teaches us that when we seek forgiveness—or we forgive others—we become more loving and compassionate towards ourselves. The bitterness and resentment we felt is eventually swept away. We begin to feel less stress and more happiness. Our outlook becomes more positive. There is also a powerful healing process that occurs within our physical and emotional Being.

This process opens the door for us to embrace the third tenet, *Taking Ownership of My Life*. It is a powerful, yet difficult, step to take because it requires us to change *how* we think. It requires us to re-examine our life in terms of what works and what doesn't work. It requires us to truly forgive ourselves for our imperfections and forgive those who have offended us in the past. Then, it challenges us to move on and leave the past in the past. *The Course of 10,000 Days®* teaches us that taking ownership of our life doesn't just happen. We must progress to that point by resolving our inner and external conflicts with others. Once we do this, we open the door for our Inner Spirit to impart love and forgiveness. And through forgiveness, healing comes.

Another passage in Dr. Kavi's book speaks to the essence of the third tenet. It reads, *"What I have experienced in my life is that I must have compassion if I expect others to be compassionate towards me. I must have forgiveness in my heart if I expect others to be merciful and forgiving towards me. I must love even my enemies if I expect to be loved. And I must take ownership of my life before I can ask others to take ownership of theirs."*

Ajay stood up, stretched out his arms and glanced at his watch. It was 12:50 pm and the afternoon ferry to Bowen Island was loading cars. "Let's make our way down to the ferry," he suggested, "and we can continue our conversation once we're aboard."

We were both stiff from sitting for nearly an hour, so we paid for our beers and walked the short distance to the ferry landing where hundreds of passengers were boarding. Two teenagers started to board ahead of an older couple and then paused to let them go ahead. "After you, please," one of them said politely. Ajay turned to me and smiled taking joy in that random act of kindness. Nothing more needed to be said. We walked aboard and made our way to the upper deck where a warm breeze crossed the bow of the ship.

We had boarded a new C-class vessel that measured 160 meters in length and could accommodate 370 vehicles. It had a capacity of nearly 1,700 passengers. But today, the ferry was operating at less than half its capacity due to the off-season. It was a beautiful new ship and we enjoyed the sunshine and warm breeze on the high deck which gave us a sweeping view of the Canadian Rockies that rose majestically along the Sea-to-Sky Highway from Horseshoe Bay to Squamish and, eventually, onto Whistler which was nestled in the mountains two hours north of Vancouver.

On Bowen Island, Ajay and I disembarked and made our way to Doc Morgan's, a popular restaurant and inn, for a late afternoon lunch. It was a quiet and restive place in mid-October since the busy tourism season had ended more than a month ago. Now, the locals on Bowen Island could relax and enjoy the tranquility.

Doc Morgan's is located in a house once owned by its namesake, a popular barber in the early days who kept his chair in the Vancouver Hotel and was known for his festive parties and crab feasts on the beach. We sat at a table that overlooked the marina and Howe Sound. Ajay wanted to sample some local wines. Our waitress, who was raised on Vancouver Island, recommended a local favorite from there, the Blue Grouse Pinot Gris. She told us it was the creation of Hans and Evangeline Kiltz who turned a wine-making hobby into a full-scale business in 1989 and created one of Vancouver Island's most elegant wine shops and tasting rooms. To this day, Ajay says that bottle of Pinot Gris was one of the best full-bodied white wines he has ever tasted. It complimented our salmon nicely.

We chatted for a while about the natural beauty of Bowen Island and the Howe Sound, but I knew from Ajay's mannerisms that he was anxious to return to our discussion about the third tenet, *Taking Ownership of One's Life*. Ajay gazed out the restaurant window to the rows of boats moored in the marina and said to me, "Gandhi said that 'our most significant battles are fought in the privacy of our own hearts.'" He let the words seep into my consciousness as I fixed my eyes on the row of sailboats in the harbor. After a moment I looked at Ajay and replied, "I think Gandhi understood better than anyone what Carl Jung meant when he wrote 'there is no coming to consciousness without pain.'"

Jung and Gandhi understood that life-changing events cause us to become reflective and introspective. Sometimes this reaction is triggered by the death of a parent or close friend. We are most vulnerable to these types of transformational experiences during our late 40s and early 50s because this period represents the end of our Fulfillment Years—our second 10,000 days. We somehow feel cheated or robbed when we lose a loved one during this period.

As we near the end of our Fulfillment Years, we begin to sense our own mortality and realize that we might not be able to achieve our greatest dreams and goals. Until that moment occurs, we falsely believe we are bullet-proof, that we can accomplish anything. Yet in the process of experiencing the loss of a loved one or some other life-changing event, we start to re-evaluate our life as we replay in our mind the lives our parents lived and our relationship with them—how they raised us and taught us; how they nurtured us or distanced themselves from us. And we compare those memories to our own parenting skills.

This reflective process, which can last years, brings to mind all the positive and negative memories of our Discovery Years. We recall the good times as well as the bad times. We remember the hardships we caused our parents. And for some reason, we dwell on our parents' failures and limitations. This is the ego's way of justifying our behavior and decisions during our Discovery Years and our Fulfillment Years. In the process of evaluating our parents *as* parents, we seek explanations for why certain things happened during our life. We wonder why our parents didn't support us more when we made certain decisions, or nurture us enough or love us enough. During this process, it's easy to assume the role of the victim-child. Frankly, some adults never grow out of this inhibiting role and debilitating mind game.

This is the painful part of coming to consciousness because there is no way we can bring back those who have died so they can help us resolve unanswered questions about our life. There is no way we can fully understand why certain things happened once our parents and loved ones are gone. We must move on and endeavor to answer these and other questions on our own. This is how the emotional legacy with our parents and loved ones is formed.

For some people it is a terribly agonizing struggle because of the pain and memories of a troubled childhood, especially for those who were abandoned, orphaned or unloved as children. For others, it's easy because their lives were normal and free of emotional turmoil with their parents.

But every person who wishes to transcend their ego and reconnect with their Inner Spirit travels this emotional and psychological road just as all the positive role models throughout history have done before us.

Ultimately, this leads us to a simple, but challenging, question: *What do I want to live for?* In order to take ownership of your life, you need to decide what you want to do with your life. What do you want to accomplish? And how will you achieve your goals and dreams? It really doesn't matter if you're 35 or 55 years old. As long as you're committed to your goals and dreams they can be realized. However, time is precious. The clock is ticking. We must act while there is still time. On this subject, Ajay shared with me a beautiful analogy he attributed to Eknath Easwaran's interpretation of the *Bhagavad Gita*. It goes like this:

> *Life is a bubble. Enjoy it while you can. Admire it. See it. Celebrate it.*
> *Because once it bursts, it will be gone forever.*
> *And all of science and technology cannot recreate that bubble.*
> *It merely becomes a drop of water.*

Satisfactorily answering the Second Sacred Question requires an in-depth self-assessment as well as deciding what you want to achieve in the next 10,000 days. The question requires us to answer it from a spiritual perspective to determine *who we are* and *what we value*; to re-connect with our Inner Spirit so we can resolve the anger, pain and wounds of the past. This is what Forgiveness is all about. But to accomplish this, we must invoke our Inner Spirit.

This is also a therapeutic process that allows us to move on and regain control of our lives so we can advance to the Third Sacred Question. For some people, the struggle with Forgiveness consumes their entire adult life. Eventually though the path leads us across the Bridge of Forgiveness. Because only by forgiving yourself and others can you reconnect with your Inner Spirit and ultimately create a purposeful life. This is the key to successfully answering the third tenet of the Second Sacred Question. It means we truly know *why* we want to live as well as the purpose and principles to which we will dedicate our life. Once we know the answers to these key questions, everything else can fall into place because we will have clarity of direction, commitment and a clean slate from which we can move forward.

Many people have asked me, "Why is forgiveness so difficult?" The answer is both simple and complex. Forgiveness, when it comes from the heart, is simple and clear. What makes the act of Forgiveness so complicated is the ego's struggle to remain in control of our thoughts and emotions. This is why our ego summons hostile emotions and negative forces to work against our Inner Spirit, and tries to prevent us from forgiving others or ourselves. I am referring to hostile forces like the four demons.

In her book, *Emotional Exorcism*, Dr. Holly A. Hunt describes the Four Demons. The Blocker Demon tries to stop us from doing positive things for ourselves. It feeds on melancholy, sadness and depression. The Negator Demon creates anxiety and worry. When we lose our car keys or find ourselves late for an appointment, it is the Negator Demon that injects stress and worry into our lives. The Rouster Demon tries to create conflict in our lives through anger and mood swings while the Tempter Demon plays on self-guilt by luring us to sabotage our life through such destructive acts and behaviors as smoking, alcohol and drug abuse.

These Four Demons are the most difficult enemies anyone can face because they pit our ego squarely against our Inner Spirit. We believe we are unworthy so we allow the Four Demons to hold us down. The more we feed them, the stronger they become. Forgiveness is the key to loosening the grip of the Four Demons and escaping their hold. Once you have crossed over the Bridge of Forgiveness, you can leave the demons behind and reach that sacred place within you where divineness dwells. *The Course* refers to this sacred place as The Kingdom of Roses.

The Course asks us to cross from one end of the Bridge of Forgiveness, which is represented by the first two tenets—*Forgiveness of Ourselves* and *Forgiveness of Others*—to the other side, which is represented by the third tenet, *Taking Ownership of My Life*. In successfully crossing over the Bridge of Forgiveness, which traverses the psychological abyss of isolation, rejection, failure and loneliness, we reach the point where self-realization and, eventually, self-actualization, can be achieved. This is how we ultimately realize our divineness.

This is a demanding process because crossing over the Bridge of Forgiveness requires us to confront our demons, not judge others and allow the Divine Source to enter our heart through our Inner Spirit and fill us with grace and peace. It requires us to acknowledge the pain and suffering we have caused others as well as release the pain we have experienced at the hands of others. Forgiveness also requires us to move beyond pain because it is not a solution, only a symptom. Forgiveness is the only meaningful solution.

When you find yourself *reacting* rather than *responding* it's important to catch yourself in these moments and ask yourself the question, *Why am I reacting this way?* If you probe deeply, you will most likely discover that your reaction is linked to one of the Four Stones: Anger, Greed, Lust and Envy. The more you practice this simple exercise, the quicker you will be able to confront those reactive moments and negative emotions that are poisoning your mind and keeping you from entering The Kingdom of Roses.

Once you embrace this concept and discover the joy of Forgiveness, your heart will be healed and the emotional and psychological barriers that prevented you from crossing the Bridge of Forgiveness will be removed. When you cross the Bridge of Forgiveness, you are within sight of The Kingdom of Roses.

Ajay and I concluded our lunch and left the warmth and comfort of Doc Morgan's restaurant on Bowen Island. We walked a short distance to the ferry landing for our trip back to Horseshoe Bay. The October wind had kicked-up and we zipped our light jackets to ward off the cool breeze that was blowing in from the northwest. Once aboard the ferry, we retreated to the upper deck behind the protection of the glass windows and peered out at the beautiful Canadian Rockies rising to the northeast and at Horseshoe Bay just off the port bow in the distance. We drank a cup of hot chocolate to warm ourselves against the cool afternoon wind that chilled the dark waters of Howe Sound and ripped through our light windbreakers.

Later that evening, after returning to Vancouver, I met with Ajay in the YEW Bar of the Four Seasons Hotel to discuss the issue of divineness and the Third Sacred Question, *How are you living a life worth remembering?*

By 9:00 pm, the bar crowd had thinned out providing a peaceful atmosphere where Ajay and I could talk openly about the conference, sample a local beer and discuss the three new assignments Ajay had given me. Rick O, who bartended at the YEW Bar for many years, recommended a locally-brewed beer called Imperial Pale Ale. It was a classic India pale ale style beer brewed by the nearby Maritime Pacific Brewing Company. We took Rick O's recommendation and he served it to us in two tulip glasses.

Ajay wanted to introduce me to the Third Sacred Question before our next meeting in Dublin, Ireland where we were scheduled to speak at another business conference. Ajay said the Third Sacred Question would be the "most challenging of the Three Sacred Questions because it would force me to confront the evils of the world and the demons within me." This statement struck me as rather harsh since I did not feel I had any demons. However, according to Ajay, "throughout life, people choose a particular path based on their values, beliefs and attitudes and sometimes that path serves good and sometimes is doesn't."

As I sat there listening to Ajay talk intensely about The Third Sacred Question and the power of evil, I wondered how this applied to me. I asked him, "Can you define 'evil?' What type of evils are you referring to?

Are we talking about things like terrorism and the holocaust?"

Ajay shook his head several times and said, "No, not at all. Acts of terrorism and the holocaust are the *result* of evil thinking. They are not the *cause*. What I am referring to are the rudimentary forms of evil that cause us to hate, kill and covet what belongs to others. I am talking about the *Four Stones*." I had heard Ajay mention the *Four Stones* before when he described his first weekend retreat with Kavi.

Ajay said, "Once you have crossed over the Bridge of Forgiveness, The Kingdom of Roses will be within sight. However, before you can pass through the gates into this sacred place where purpose, peace and passion are found, you must overturn the Four Stones that block the entrance."

CHAPTER 20

The Four Stones

B efore we can cleanse our hearts and experience our human divineness, we must confront the Four Stones—Anger, Greed, Lust and Envy—and cross over the Bridge of Forgiveness. *The Course* teaches us that every human being carries the weight of the Four Stones to some degree. While there are other hardships that weigh us down, The Four Stones keep us from achieving purpose, peace and passion in our life. This is why we must overcome them before the Divine Source will allow us to experience The Kingdom of Roses.

The size and burden of our Four Stones varies depending on how significant a role each one plays in our life. For some people, it takes 10,000 days to overturn their stones. Ultimately, the time required to overturn the Four Stones depends on your commitment to discovering your higher purpose and the intensity of your desire to enter The Kingdom of Roses. According to *The Course*, we have 10,000 days—our Legacy Years—to figure it out and transform ourselves so we can attain inner peace and live our higher purpose. Every problem we encounter, every serious illness we suffer and every war that has ever been fought can be attributed directly to one or more of the Four Stones because they are so deeply ingrained in our physical, emotional and mental states.

"For some people it takes a lifetime to overturn their Four Stones. Actually, the time required to overturn the Four Stones depends on the results people want to achieve in their lifetime," Ajay told me. "*The Course* gives us 10,000 days to figure it all out and redirect our lives so that we can attain inner peace and live our higher purpose in this lifetime."

I asked Ajay what role, if any, our Inner Spirit played in this process. Ajay replied, "In each person's life, there are several opportunities to hear your Inner Spirit and respond. When you open your heart to that calling, your Inner Spirit will surface and begin to work its special powers. In my case, I had one of those 'ah-ha' moments ten years ago while attending our annual corporate leadership meeting. In fact, it was the reason you and I first met!"

I asked Ajay to tell me the story.

As he drank his Imperial Pale Ale, Ajay said, "It was during our annual spring leadership retreat in Palm Springs and I had just met privately with Bob Tohmy, our CEO, who complimented my on my performance and numbers. Then Bob suggested I get a leadership coach. I gave him the usual courteous response but never acted on his suggestion.

"But the next year at our leadership retreat in Pebble Beach, we had the same conversation. 'Great results, Ajay,' Bob told me, 'but you could really use a leadership coach.' I was somewhat vexed by his suggestion this time, so I asked him why he thought I needed a leadership coach when my numbers and performance were superior to all the other division presidents in the company.

"Bob's answer stopped me dead in my tracks. He told me, 'It's not about your numbers, Ajay. It's about your ability to command respect and inspire people. Frankly, for you, it's attitudinal. You have the potential to lead this company someday. But you need to work on your relationship-building skills. If you aspire to get to the next level, you're going to have to spend some time learning how to control your ego and consider the needs of others who will serve you. It's a question of your ability to positively relate to others. If you're interested, I know someone outside the company who can help you. Let me know if you want his name and phone number.'

"Relationship building and attitudinal issues? Ego? What the hell was Bob talking about? I couldn't believe my ears. I felt offended and wanted to storm out of the room at that very moment. After all, I was the fair-haired boy at TGC. I was out-performing everyone; and yet, my CEO was telling me I needed to get 'unstuck?' I wasn't stuck! He was dead wrong. Later that evening, as I walked along the village shops on Ocean Avenue in Carmel, I began to ask myself some serious questions about how I related to people and if, perhaps, my ego was in control. Despite acknowledging a few instances where several of my direct reports seemed to be distancing themselves from me and avoiding me when it came to tough issues, I still wasn't convinced that Bob was correct in his evaluation of me.

"The next day I had my watershed moment—the kind of moment that transforms one's life. We had adjourned for the afternoon to have a few beers and watch the NCAA basketball tournament's Final Four games on television. Most of the TGC team had gathered in The Tap Room to watch the games. Indiana University's basketball team was playing. Their coach was the colorful Bobby Knight who had a reputation for winning, but also prowling the sidelines and ranting at his players and the officials. Bobby was on an emotional tirade that evening—kicking chairs, yelling at the officials and getting worked-up about a bad call they had made against his team.

"The TV commentators noted Knight's sideline tantrum and remarked that he would draw a technical foul if he didn't regain his composure. At this point, Bob Tohmy, who was sitting next to me at the bar, leaned over and said quietly, 'Ajay, that's what I was talking about earlier! Sometimes you remind your employees of Bobby Knight!'

"I was stunned. Before I could reply, Bob had slipped away to greet one of the Pebble Beach owners who had walked into The Tap Room. 'Was I *that* bad?' I asked myself. I didn't sleep well that night because my mind struggled with the deeper, unspoken message my CEO was tactfully conveying. Despite my outstanding results, my career with TGC was in jeopardy because I was emotionally out of balance. It was at that moment that I had my epiphany.

"It wasn't my *results* my CEO was worried about. It was my *methods*. By using the metaphor of a confrontational, but successful college basketball coach, Bob Tohmy was telling me, 'Yes, Ajay, you are winning and getting results, but your *approach* to the game of business is taking a serious human toll and alienating the very people you care about the most—your employees, colleagues and key suppliers. We can't afford to lose all three of them and keep you!'

"I didn't realize it, but I was slowly losing my support base; and the only option left for my boss—short of firing me—was to get me help through a leadership coach. I felt empty inside. For nearly two years, I had ignored the signals; and now, I was wondering if it might be too late. Of course, that's how I met you, Tom. You were the leadership coach that Bob Tohmy recommended."

I told Ajay I remember getting Bob's phone call giving me a heads-up that he might be calling.

Ajay drank his beer and added, "Well, the next morning, before our closing session, I made a point to speak with Bob and told him I had thought about his suggestion. I was ready to make the necessary changes and I appreciated his patience and faith in me during the past two years. He put his arm on my shoulder, smiled and said, 'I'm glad to hear that, Ajay. I think it will make a major difference for you.'"

Ajay finished his beer and said to me, "Little did I know that two years later I would reconnect with my boyhood friend, Kavi, and experience *The Course of 10,000 Days*®! So, as you can imagine, it's been an amazing time for me."

After Ajay shared his story, I reminded him of our first meeting and how I compared Bobby Knight's management style to that of UCLA Basketball Coach John Wooden's management style—not knowing that Bob Tohmy had used a similar analogy.

"Yes, as a matter of fact," Ajay noted, "I vividly remember our first meeting in Irvine and how you reminded me that anyone who wins twelve NCAA Basketball championships is probably a *God*, not a coach. But, you know what? I think I've become more like Coach Wooden over the past seven years because I've focused more on my players and less on me.

"I began to take a greater personal interest in them as people as well as their issues and challenges in order to earn their trust. And I still have that little blue book you gave me to read by Coach Wooden, *The Pyramid of Success*. As I think back on those early days in our relationship, it's interesting that you would have cited Coach Wooden's philosophy as a role model for me. After all, it's basic and simple, but it certainly works in sports and business. I think that's one reason why Coach Wooden won so many basketball games over the years. He focused on the basics of the game and kept things simple for his players. You might say he emphasized the *vital few* instead of getting lost in the *trivial many*!"

"While that's true," I acknowledged, "I think he also earned the adoration of his university and the respect of every die-hard basketball fan in America because of his professional attitude and mature approach to the game."

Fifteen months after I started working with Ajay as his leadership coach, he enrolled in Kavi's weekend retreat for *The Course*. A month later, Kavi had Ajay practicing the BAG IT exercise and observing birds in his backyard. Ajay also began to take mid-day breaks in TGC's corporate park which was adjacent to his office building. I reminded Ajay that we used to have some of our coaching sessions in TGC's corporate park by the lake.

"That's right," Ajay replied. "Every afternoon at 2:00 pm, I blocked a half hour for reflection time and walked down the path and sat on that weathered gray bench by the lake for 15 minutes. I opened up a small plastic bag of bird seed and fed the birds and squirrels."

Rick O, the bartender, brought us two more Imperial Pale Ale beers. Ajay took a sip from his tulip glass and continued his story. "Soon after I started this, I noticed other managers taking a few minutes out of their day to clear their heads as they walked around the lake. Some guys even brought bird seed to the park to feed the birds. I think it helped them relax and ease their minds. It also created a positive environment for innovative thinking and problem solving. It's interesting to note that shortly after people saw me taking an afternoon break by walking around the lake, more employees began to enjoy our corporate park and the lake. In fact, I think it's the reason we started getting better ideas. People were able to relax more and clear their heads. And, our results improved!

"At first, I think Bob was intrigued by the number of employees who were walking around the lake. He didn't say anything except to comment that he was pleased 'everyone was getting some physical exercise and fresh air.' I do recall a few months later, he invited me to take a stroll around the lake with him. That was a first! We had a great conversation about life, my progress with you as my leadership coach and my initial participation in *The Course*. I think Bob was intrigued by it as well as the progress I was making as a person and a leader. So, that encouraged me to continue my new routine and spend more time mastering *The Course*."

Then, in a reflective tone, Ajay looked at me and said, "But I still had to overcome the Four Stones in order to enter The Kingdom of Roses. Kavi taught me that every problem we encounter on this planet, every illness we suffer, every war that will ever be fought, can be attributed directly to the Four Stones because they are so deeply rooted in our culture and persona.

"*The Course* teaches us that our feelings and emotions, including hatred and the Negative Three R's, are based on a false sense of fear. And this fear stems from misleading values and beliefs we were taught as young children that 'those people' will do us harm. I'm not referring to thieves and murderers, but people who dress differently, or worship differently or have a different skin color than us. Because of these mistaken beliefs, we automatically revert to our biases and prejudices that have never been properly challenged through a process of self-examination or personal reflection. We remain ignorant by accepting these beliefs as true when, in fact, they are unfounded. This is why many societies react in insane ways when their 'fear button' is pushed.

"Think about it," Ajay continued. "This sense of fear and misguided beliefs are the root cause of most tribal wars and religious strife in Africa, South America and the Middle East. It was even the root cause for America's Civil War. If only America's Founding Fathers had the courage to do the right thing in 1776 and abolish slavery, we would have been spared that costly war. But because of greed, fear and the social norms of the day, people justified slavery. There are too many dictators and governments that oppress people and deny them their God-given rights because they are driven by anger, greed, lust and envy. People are sick and tired of oppression. This explains what's happening in countries like Egypt, Tunisia, Libya and other countries.

"Unfortunately," Ajay added, "despite more than two hundred years of freedom and democracy in America, we still struggle with bigotry and racism in our own country. I came to the United States at the age of 23 and became a citizen seven years later. Yet I can tell you that some of my fellow citizens do not consider me to be an equal among them despite the fact that I vote, I pay a significant amount of personal income tax, I own a home in Newport Beach and my company pays hundreds of millions of dollars annually in corporate taxes. And for what it's worth, I work hard to make sure that our 75,000 employees are well paid, trained and able to contribute to their communities. Yet, for some people, I am still an outsider —an Indian because my skin is brown not white. Why is it that people are so shallow and so bigoted?"

I could see the frustration and emotion in Ajay's eyes as he spoke about his personal dealings with discrimination and the insensitivity of certain people. Despite Ajay's success and contributions to his company and community, the 'outsider' label still hurt him.

I took advantage of the pause in our conversation to ask a question. "So, how do we confront our demons and change how we think? How do we reach those ignorant and bigoted people and help them to elevate their thinking?"

Ajay reflected on my question as he drank his beer and gazed out the large picture window onto downtown Vancouver's Georgia Street where a steady stream of people walked by the bar enjoying the mild October evening.

"You realize we're talking about our neighbors as well as ourselves, don't you?" Ajay asked with a cracked smile and a degree of sarcasm in his voice. I nodded my head and smiled knowing there was much truth in what Ajay had just told me.

He continued. "Well, according to Kavi, there needs to be a new consciousness. This is why *The Course of 10,000 Days*® has such relevance and a sense of urgency. Time is ticking away for all of us. Society needs to awaken to the reality that our world cannot continue on its present course and expect to survive. We need to fashion a higher standard of living for all people and hold governments accountable to those standards because all people are entitled to certain human rights and the opportunity to pursue their dreams."

After pausing for a long moment, Ajay added, "Let me share with you an example that Kavi offered during our first weekend retreat. Consider how the nations of the world would react if the Earth was under the threat of annihilation from some supernatural force. Would we continue to wage war against each other or would we unite our resources and talents to avoid Armageddon? When I was a boy, I saw an American science fiction movie, *The Day the Earth Stood Still*. Its message was 'live in peace or a higher civilization will eliminate your planet.' If we were ever faced with that ultimatum, I wonder if warring nations would come to their senses and find a solution because the consequences would be just too horrible to fathom. In the final analysis, most nations and societies share the same values and goals. While our approaches to governing vary considerably, all people desire freedom and the pursuit of happiness.

"This is why Kavi is such a strong advocate of a new consciousness around the world; a consciousness that has political and spiritual overtones. Kavi taught me, and I am teaching you, that we are all children of the Divine Source. Therefore, we all deserve the right to live in peace and pursue our dreams. Jesus understood this when he said, 'Let him who is without sin cast the first stone.' If we desire to attain our higher purpose, we must first understand our weaknesses and work together to create a better world. This is the only way I know of that we can ensure the survival of our civilization."

As Ajay spoke, I could see a deep fire in his eyes I had not seen before. His eyes watered as he told me his experiences with discrimination and the *Four Stones*. "I have visited many countries and spoken to the local people," Ajay noted. "I have drunk wine in their villages and eaten rice on the dirt floors of their huts. I can tell you that without exception, all people yearn for peace and freedom. Everyone's heart is filled with dreams. We want to see our children grow and live to see our grandchildren have a joyful and abundant life. We want to live a purposeful life and experience the glory of a beautiful sunrise and the joy of living a life worth remembering.

"Why can't we live in a world of peace, enjoy our freedom and love each other? There is only one reason: The Four Stones. Regrettably, too many people have been poisoned by hate, fear, revenge and war. Their hearts have been hardened by the Four Stones of Anger, Greed, Lust and Envy. Since civilization began, corrupt leaders have led people down the wrong path using the Four Stones as their psychological weapon. In the end, death and destruction become their epithets. Ironically, today's society faces the same perils despite advances in technology, medicine, energy, science and thought. This is why The Kingdom of Roses belongs only to those who have overturned the Four Stones, purified their hearts and discovered their higher purpose.

"Until our world leaders learn that it is easier to forgive and find common ground by which we can all live together, the consequences of evil will be with us and innocent people will suffer. Unless societies rise up—as my birth nation of India did in the 1940s by following the non-violent principles of Gandhi—and challenge this insanity, the ultimate evil of nuclear Armageddon will end civilization as we know it. The choice is ours, but we have less than 10,000 days to take action and change the way we think and act. Each person must decide for himself because each person has a stake in our planet's future."

I hung on every word Ajay spoke. I had never heard him express himself in such a personal and articulate manner about the need for a higher consciousness and a new level of inspired global leadership for our world. It moved me.

Ajay took a long sip of his Imperial Pale Ale and then said to me, "This is why the Third Sacred Question is so difficult. You cannot find love if your heart is filled with hatred. You cannot experience love if you are greedy, corrupt, bent on revenge or lust for power in order to exercise control over the lives of people. In essence, you cannot master *The Course* and enter The Kingdom of Roses without carefully examining your heart and redefining your values and beliefs. Only when those things are in alignment with your Inner Spirit will it be possible to overturn The Four Stones."

As Ajay sipped his beer, I asked him how we could change how society thinks and acts. "The challenge almost seems impossible," I said with a deep sigh.

Ajay anticipated my question and responded quickly. "Well, you're right in the sense that we are all human and, therefore, we are prone to repeat the same mistakes. For example, look at how many wars we fight. This is partly due to the fact that we cling to corrupt values and misguided beliefs instead of replacing them with values centered on love, trust, generosity and empathy for all human beings.

"Having said that, we cannot be naïve. There are evil-doers in this world and that will always be the case. Not every human being subscribes to the values of peace and love. This is why America must always remain vigilant and have a dominant military force. But, we must also use it prudently. For better or for worse, America has become the protector of democracy, the champion of peace and freedom's advocate around the world. No other nation is willing to make that sacrifice for freedom; and yet, too often we are ridiculed for it."

Ajay's response led me to ask if he thought America was being criticized for certain military actions or because our political motives appeared less than honorable.

He smiled and said, "Well, therein lies our nation's dilemma. We need to be prudent politically and militarily. President Eisenhower, a retired five-star general, cautioned us against the military industrial complex before he left office. Eisenhower had a valid concern because he knew there were unscrupulous people who would get rich from war. It didn't matter to them if human beings suffered or died. Their greed and conceit took precedence. Nevertheless, there are many ways each day you and I can practice positive virtues, don't you agree?

"For example, I like the bumper sticker that encourages people to 'perform random acts of kindness and reckless acts of civility.' You might recall earlier today we talked about civility. Civility is really just another form of kindness. In effect, civility is a loving act of kindness towards other human beings. It's empathy in action. And each act of kindness we perform also makes us feel good. It also counters an act of evil somewhere in the world and helps us turn over The Four Stones that prevent us from entering The Kingdom of Roses."

As I finished my beer, I asked Ajay how I could respond to the Third Sacred Question when I know I'm imperfect.

"Do not confuse perfection with consciousness," Ajay counseled. "What *The Course* teaches us is to question old beliefs and values. Each time you find yourself being less than kind, using harsh language with someone or running out of patience with a bad driver on the road or long lines in the grocery store, this is an opportunity for you to simply stop, take a deep breath and say to yourself, 'My approach is unkind. Try a different approach, one based on love and understanding.' Then, try to express yourself in a different way. When you do this, it reinforces your commitment to the second tenet of the Second Sacred Question and opens up The Kingdom of Roses for you.

"We need to calm our mind and emotions and listen to our negative words," Ajay noted. "Because *how* you express yourself will determine how others *react* and *respond* to you. But there is another dimension here that you need to be aware of, and it is this. You also should want to understand what *causes* you to react this way?

"Remember in Laguna Beach when we first began this journey, we discussed the importance of 'not *reacting*, but rather, *responding.*' It's important to catch yourself in these moments and ask yourself the question, *Why am I reacting this way?* If you probe deeply, you will most likely discover that your reaction is linked to one of The Four Stones. The more you practice this simple exercise, the quicker you will be able to confront those false beliefs and negative values that are poisoning your mind and keeping you from entering The Kingdom of Roses."

Ajay then turned his attention to my three new assignments. He told me my first assignment was to purchase a bird feeder and observe the birds' behavior and interaction. *The Course* teaches that reflection is an action. It creates awareness which places you in communion with the whole of life. Listening and observing are two of the most effective reflection techniques.

The second assignment was to practice the "BAG It" Exercise. Every morning, I was to think of three blessings in my life. The B is for Blessings. Next, I had to think of three accomplishments I had achieved during the past 24 hours. The A is for Accomplishments. Finally, I had to set three goals. The G is for Goals. They didn't have to be major goals. In fact, I was instructed to make them simple goals so when I awoke the following morning and performed my "BAG IT" exercise, today's Goals would become tomorrow's Accomplishments.

My third assignment was to study roses. Ajay instructed me to visit a nursery or garden store and learn about roses. He also told me these exercises were designed to quiet my ego, allow time for reflection so that my Inner Spirit could surface and begin the process of expelling my demons.

I agreed to start all three assignments immediately when I returned to San Diego so Ajay and I could discuss my progress when we met again in a few weeks.

It was getting late and we decided to end our conversation at this point. Before leaving, Ajay gave me a few additional words of advice in understanding the Third Sacred Question as well as the Bridge of Forgiveness and The Four Stones. We also reconfirmed our plans to meet in Dublin where we would both be speaking at the World Congress of International Corporations to be held at Dublin's beautiful new convention center.

Ajay had given me so much to think about I found it hard to sleep. I awoke the next morning and after exercising for 45 minutes, I showered and ate a light breakfast. Then, I took a taxi to the Vancouver airport for my flight to San Diego. Ajay had left earlier that morning for New York to meet with his CEO and brief Wall Street analysts on the company's fourth quarter forecasts and year-to-date performance.

CHAPTER 21

The Third Sacred Question

W hen I returned to San Diego the following morning, it was a beautiful autumn day and the sun was melting the morning dew as it glistened on the fairways of Mt. Woodson golf course. I retrieved my shillelagh and began my morning walk. I looked at the white business card Ajay had given me in Vancouver and read it. On the front was the Third Sacred Question with the symbolic red rose in the upper left corner. It read: *How are you living a life worth remembering?*

I turned over the business card and read the three tenets of the Third Sacred Question.

> *How do you demonstrate your love of self?*
> *How do you demonstrate your love for other people and all living things?*
> *What have you done today to contribute to a better tomorrow?*

As I walked down the empty 18th fairway, I asked myself, *"How do I demonstrate love of self?"* This first tenet required me to move beyond all personal judgments and negative responses about myself. I needed to acknowledge that despite my limitations, weaknesses and inadequacies it was important for me to appreciate myself for who I am. This question caused me to wrestle with the deeper issues of self-respect, self-worth and genuine self-love—issues that must be explored, according to Ajay, if I wanted to experience my divineness in this lifetime.

During this time of year, a thick marine layer often blows inland from the Pacific Ocean and settles 20 miles east of Del Mar on Mt. Woodson golf course until the morning sun breaks through and burns it off. It created an eerie contrast as I walked the course. Above me, I could see blue sky and the rugged boulders jutting out of Mt. Woodson, which rises 2,850 feet above sea level. Ahead of me, the fairways were shrouded in a thick, misty morning fog. I realized the answer to the Third Sacred Question was like the path ahead. I would have to trust my instincts to find my way step-by-step and, eventually, the answers would reveal themselves to me.

As I continued on my morning walk, I recalled an earlier discussion I had with Ajay about living a life worth remembering and maintaining a balanced life. Ajay shared with me the Indian philosophy dealing with the four main goals of life: Kama, Dharma, Artha and Moksha. Ajay noted that in Eastern philosophy all things are interconnected; therefore, we are one. Human beings are part of this *oneness* because we are part of the whole. We cannot function separate and apart from nature or the universe. As *The Course* teaches, as we find purpose, peace and passion in our life, the value of our life experience is enhanced. This is how we live a life worth remembering.

Kama is the enjoyment of the five senses—hearing, feeling, seeing, tasting and smelling. While it is often associated with the erotic nature of sexual pleasures, Kama also seeks to bring the mind together with the soul to create the consciousness of pleasure.

Dharma is virtuous living and selfless service to others. It represents the humanitarian qualities within each human being. *The Course* reminds us that to live a life worth remembering we must serve others and help those who can benefit from our gifts. This is how we live our higher purpose.

Artha is the life goal relating to materialism and worldly success. As *The Course* teaches, there is nothing wrong with the accumulation of wealth so long as we use it properly and not transgress. It is not necessary to choose between God and material goods; both have their place. Money is merely a byproduct of one's time, energy and talent well spent.

Moksha is the life goal that releases us from the cycle of death and rebirth by awakening our Inner Spirit so we can transcend our earthly existence.

According to the mystic teachings, of the first three, Dharma (virtue) is the highest goal. Artha (a secure life) ranks second, and Kama (pleasure) is the least important. Together with all these, there is also the aspiration for *Moksha*, the attainment of God, which is a fulfillment of the whole complex of desires, physical as well as spiritual. When your motives clash, the higher ideal is to be followed. Thus, when it comes to making money, virtue must not be compromised. However, earning a living should take precedence over pleasure.

Part Three

Acceptance of the Divine

CHAPTER 22

The Divine Source

Access to the Divine Source is possible through our intellect, imagination and creativity. We manifest our divineness every day through our music, artistry, innovations and mastery of discovery. Divineness is a concept that is beyond the grasp of most people for two reasons.

First, we have been taught that only God is divine. Secondly, we have been taught that human beings are made in the image and likeness of God. However, just the opposite is true. It is not God who made us in its image and likeness, rather it is mankind who has created God in *our* image and likeness. If we had truly been made in God's image and likeness, we would remain perfect beings in every respect since the concept of God denotes perfection and, therefore, God would create nothing less than perfection.

This explains why we have been taught that mankind is flawed and only God is divine. It is contrary to most religious doctrine—not to mention our own belief system—to think that human beings also have divine potential. This is why it is extremely difficult for human beings to understand or perceive the principle of human divineness. So we blindly accept the faulty reasoning that only God is divine. But, as *The Course* teaches us, this is not the case.

Furthermore, we have a parochial understanding of God. When asked to define or describe God, most people will say the Almighty is a stern, old white man with wavy white hair and a thick white beard. Of course, this is how Michelangelo di Lodovico Buonarroti Simoni depicted God in his famous Sistine Chapel paintings. If only people knew that Michelangelo cast an old street vendor in Rome for his model of God, they might have second thoughts about who God really is and what he looks like!

This brings us to a crucial point in terms of *The Course* and its views on God and religion. Because the concept of the Divine Source and the role of religion play such an important part in our lives, it is essential to move beyond the myths about God. The Bible and other respected ancient teachings on this subject only represent the tip of the iceberg in terms of unmasking the truth about the Divine Source and our untapped human potential. This is why *The Course* encourages us to probe deeper by challenging the status quo as well as our own beliefs and values on these subjects.

The Course suggests that all our beliefs and values should undergo scrutiny in order to connect with our Inner Spirit and attain our higher purpose. Until we do so, the truth will remain cloaked in legends, myths and man-made religious dogma. As mythologist Joseph Campbell so eloquently describes in his writings, much of what western civilization currently believes about God is based on Greek and Roman mythology instead of rational thinking and our life experiences. In essence, our ignorance about the Divine Source and mankind's lack of vision inhibit us from achieving our divineness on earth.

The Course teaches us that a Divine Source exists, but it is beyond the comprehension of most human beings because it has rarely been experienced or witnessed. Nevertheless, the Divine Source surrounds us and penetrates us. Joseph Campbell says the Divine Source is a "universal energy—a wholeness—a force so powerful that it is responsible for the creation of all things. It binds us together and creates order out of chaos. The planets and universe are part of its creation."

Fortunately, the Divine Source has given us the necessary resources to survive and thrive on Earth, but it does not interfere with the natural order nor does it change water into wine or perform miracles. However, this is not to say that mankind cannot use its powers to shape or alter the course of its destiny—for better or for worse. While we possess the same potential as the Divine Source, we manifest that potential differently because of our limited thinking and lack of enlightenment. Nevertheless, our divineness continues to be channeled through our thoughts, behaviors, vision and actions. We simply fail to recognize it as such.

Unfortunately, people have been duped for centuries by manipulative institutions that discourage us from thinking on a higher level. They tell us we are not worthy of attaining divineness because we have been stained with sin since our birth. Such claims are a fabrication of unscrupulous leaders who simply seek power and control over humanity.

Ironically, the greatest proof of humanity's divineness is Jesus, the most recognized symbol of Christianity. If Jesus was, in fact, human and capable of attaining divineness, why can't other human beings? Some might retort that the answer to this question is simple: Jesus is the son of God! But, if we accept that argument, does it not make sense that we are *all* sons (and daughters) of God?

Why would God single out one human being at the exclusion of all others? It doesn't make sense when you consider the infinite powers and wisdom of the Divine Source. This is why mythology and logic are important factors in completing the equation of the Divine Source. As human beings, we must be able to differentiate mythology from logic and separate faith from fiction.

The Course teaches us three things about religion. First, while the question of whether or not God made man can be doubted and debated, there is no doubt that man created God. It is a fact that for millenniums mankind has worshipped many types of Gods—from the sun to Zeus, from golden cows to Biblical creations depicting God as a stern, old man with flowing white hair and a beard.

Second, all religion is a fabrication of man. The reason mankind created religion is because we are a weak and frail species when it comes to believing in ourselves. We do not have sufficient faith in our talents and capabilities. Consider the fact that it has taken us more than 100,000 years to progress from the invention of fire to the point where we can use our mind powers to walk across a bed of burning coals. And because of our emotional frailty, mankind needed to create a God figure that would give us hope, inspiration and courage.

For this very reason, men created religions so that like-minded people, who shared a common belief system and embraced certain traditions, rituals and worship preferences, could do so together. This is how religious communities initially were formed and organized religion came into existence.

Third, as religions and empires became established, they needed to solidify their standing among society to ensure their survival and dominance. Thus, religions created their own hierarchy, rules, sacraments, commandments, rituals, gospels and penance—to cultivate allegiance and maintain control over the uncleansed masses. Ironically, over the ages, millions of people have been tortured, killed, imprisoned, punished and banished by organized religion in order to demonstrate their indomitable power and authority.

While many people profess to be Christians, few Christians know that Emperor Constantine and his successors in the 4th Century AD shaped the Christian doctrine as we know it today. Historical accounts tell us that the original doctrine, rituals and practices set forth by the Apostle Paul and other disciples of Jesus were changed dramatically by Constantine. The emperor also established a church hierarchy of his own design and he established a set of beliefs and practices which remain today as the basis for all mainstream Bible-based churches.

Furthermore, Constantine began a centuries-long effort to eliminate any book in the original Bible considered *unacceptable* to his *revised* doctrine of the church. At that time, it is believed there were up to 600 books that comprised the work we know today as the Bible. Through a series of decisions made by church leaders during Constantine's time and subsequent reigns, all but 80 of those 600 books, known today as the King James Translation of 1611, were purged from the work. There was a further reduction by the Protestant Reformation bringing the number to 66 in the authorized King James Bible.

Given this historical account of how organized religion evolved over the centuries, it is easy to see how the words and teachings of Jesus were muddled by well-intentioned men. It also reinforces the argument that most established religions are not based on the word of God, but rather the whims of Emperor Constantine and his minions who rewrote the teachings of the early Christian church and gave it its current structure.

Despite all this, *The Course* teaches that Jesus demonstrated his divineness through his thoughts, behavior, acts of kindness, love and forgiveness. Throughout all the gospels—not just the four that were sanctioned by King Constantine—Jesus reminds us that we should follow his example and aspire to reach a higher plateau of understanding and self-fulfillment. This is accomplished through our Inner Spirit. So if Jesus, a human being who walked the earth just as we do today, can do it, so can any human being because we possess the same qualities and attributes Jesus did. In fact, the underlying theme of Jesus' teachings was "do as I do and you can attain the same results."

Still, there are those who argue divineness is the exclusive purview of God. Unfortunately, there is no worse condition for a man to be in than to think he knows when, in fact, he is ignorant. His arrogance prevents him from ever truly knowing or learning the truth or separating fact from fiction.

The matter of accepting our divineness comes down to faith and trust. For those enlightened few who have experienced an ethereal awakening and understand the infinite power and energy of our universe, embracing the concept of the Divine Source and our ability to attain divineness in our lifetime is both real and doable.

Also, it's important not to confuse perfection with consciousness. As Carl Jung wrote, "Wholeness does not mean perfection." The reason *The Course* encourages us to question our beliefs and values as we mature is to be sure they are still valid. Why? Because we are not the same person at age 45 that we were at age 25. Not only do our bodies change, but so do our thoughts, beliefs, values and convictions. And so should our hearts.

Ray Kroc, the venerable founder of McDonald's had it right when he said, "People are like bananas. We're either green and ripening or yellow and rotting!" *The Course* recognizes that people and their environments change. Our relationships also change and, over time, so might our beliefs and values because we become wiser and, hopefully, enlightened. As we grow older, we see the world through different colored glasses—a fresh perspective, if you will.

This brings us back to Plato's *The Phaedo* and its relationship to proving the existence of the Divine Source. In Plato's story, Socrates explains to his friends that acquiring knowledge comes from a recollection of experiences from a previous life. Based on this premise, according to Socrates, if human beings can learn anything, they must have known *something* about what it is they are learning. If a human being has known something without having been taught it (in this lifetime), they must have learned it before their birth. If the soul existed prior to birth, it stands to reason that it survives death.

Therefore, Socrates' friends had no cause for grief as the great philosopher prepared to carry out his own execution by drinking hemlock. This prior knowledge is triggered into consciousness by sensory input or, as Plato believed, a Divine Source. In writing *The Phaedo*, Plato attempted to unmask the paradox of what is known and unknown; and, the source of human knowledge which Plato believed originates from a higher power. Thus, for Plato, the existence of the Divine Source is not a question of faith or trust, but a matter of reason.

CHAPTER 23

Like and Love

As I continued my morning walk, I thought about the first tenet of the Third Sacred Question: *How do you demonstrate your love of self?* I recalled a quote from author Paul Mauchline who said, "The degree to which you love yourself is the degree to which you will be able to extend love to others."

I also recalled what *The Course* teaches about the differences between *like* and *love*. *Like* is how you *feel* about someone but *love* is how you *treat* them. Instinctively, people know whether you *like* them or *love* them by the way you treat them.

During *The Course* retreats, Dr. Kavi often quoted the lyrics of John Lennon and Paul McCartney, which he believes complements the Third Sacred Question. Dr. Kavi enjoys the Beatles' music because it is filled with unfettered optimism and love themes. Dr. Kavi's favorite Beatles' lyric is tied directly to the first tenet: "And in the end, the love you take is equal to the love you make." I thought about this lyric as I asked myself how I demonstrated love of self.

The Course teaches us that love is something that must be learned and relearned with each new encounter, with each new relationship. Kavi frequently quotes author Erich Fromm who wrote, "Love is an art that requires patience, confidence, discipline, concentration, faith and practice daily."

One of the books Dr. Kavi recommends to students of *The Course* is Erich Fromm's *The Art of Loving*. This is required reading for anyone who wants to truly master the Third Sacred Question. *The Course* teaches us that self-love is healthy. According to Fromm, "The love for my own self is inseparably connected with the love for any other being." *The Course* reminds us that love is an attitude *and* an action. It also is the root of the Four Goals of Life—Kama, Artha, Dharma and Moksha—which I mentioned in an earlier chapter.

Dr. Kavi's favorite passage from Fromm's book describes love as the ability to give. Dr. Kavi tells his students that Fromm understood the internal struggle of self-love and ego. Fromm also understood the difficulties most people have with being alone and at peace with their aloneness.

In his journal, Ajay wrote the following note based on what he had learned from Dr. Kavi during *The Course* retreat:

> *Kavi counseled his students on self-love and discussed the relevance of Fromm's writings. Kavi said, "How could anyone consider self-love to be narcissistic—as Freud suggested—when you realize that a selfish person is only interested in himself, not others. The selfish person wants control over others. He covets the possessions of others. He gets no pleasure from giving, but only in taking. Fromm believes, as I do, that selfishness and self-love are not identical. They are, in fact, opposites. The harsh truth is that selfish persons are not capable of loving others; but they are also not capable of loving themselves. On these points, Fromm and the teachings of The Course are in complete harmony. So long as you deny yourself love and the ability to love yourself, you deny yourself of your divineness.*

Many people have a difficult time with the concept of being alone. I'm not talking about loneliness or isolation, but rather the simple concept of time spent with yourself—just being alone. We live in a world in which group identity and social networking is over-emphasized albeit very important in terms of how people communicate. We have become reliant and dependent on our family, friends, work associates, church, school, bridge club, golf partners and often our spouses. Very few people value being alone and being apart from the group. This makes the notion of self-love even more difficult to accept because society equates *aloneness* with personal problems, isolationism or mental disorder. It's simply not viewed as a normal behavior pattern.

One of the issues you will struggle with in answering the Third Sacred Question is how does the individual maintain his uniqueness, his oneness, despite the pressure to conform and be part of the whole of society? As Fromm wrote, "An individual can never discover his higher purpose if all his time is spent engaged in group think." The deeper issue here deals with how do we preserve time alone so we can explore our uniqueness, our oneness? Self-love cannot blossom or mature if the individual has no sense of self-appreciation or does not value his own lovable attributes.

One quiet afternoon, I took a break from work and walked across the street to a park where I sat on a bench to contemplate the second tenet of the Third Sacred Question: *How do you demonstrate your love for other people and all living things?* This was a challenging question because, frankly, there were some people and living things I didn't love. For example, Osama bin Laden, Hitler, spiders, rattlesnakes and gophers in my front yard! Perhaps I was misinterpreting the second tenet. Then, it occurred to me that perhaps I was limiting my thoughts to my ego's definition of *love* rather than a broader interpretation of what the second tenet was really asking. Eventually, I realized the second tenet was not asking me to unconditionally love evil persons or embrace their ideologies. I had missed the essence of the question. What the second tenet was challenging me to do was to stop judging people based on inconclusive evidence and first emotions. It was asking me to control my ego's response and discover kindness, understanding, forgiveness, empathy and compassion for those people and things I disliked.

I smiled to myself as I recalled a bumper sticker that read, *When Jesus said, "Love Thy Enemy," what he probably meant was don't kill them!*

Each day we encounter—directly and indirectly—people we don't particularly like as well as situations that push our buttons and cause us to react negatively. This is why *The Course of 10,000 Days*® reinforces the Law of Cause and Effect which states that for every action, there is a reaction; and, for every reaction, there should be a thoughtful response. That response should be one of understanding, compassion, forgiveness and love whenever possible. If we do not give, we cannot receive. If we do not seek to understand, we remain blinded by our ignorance and biases. If we do not love, we will not be loved in return. If we do not forgive, we will not be forgiven. If we are not kind and merciful to others, the cosmos somehow has a way of making ours days more difficult.

I know it's hard to change beliefs, values, behaviors and attitudes. We easily get set in our ways. We grow comfortable with ourselves, our grudges, our animosity for contrary ideologies and our negative feelings for certain people and things. In fact, we become so comfortable living with our negativity that we don't realize it. But, if we want to discover our higher purpose, we must challenge the way we currently see things and take the necessary steps to improve our lives so our Inner Spirit can surface and guide us to The Kingdom of Roses.

By practicing the virtues of compassion, forgiveness and kindness, we learn *how* to love all persons and all living things. We learn how to be merciful towards those who have offended us. Ultimately, this will help us discover our divineness. Love and forgiveness are the foundation of our divineness and the keys to entering The Kingdom of Roses.

The Course encourages us to embrace all people in an effort to help us overturn our Four Stones. This is why society's efforts and commitment to diversity of thought and embracing all people is essential. We need to learn how to be uncomfortable with people who are different than us in order to one day embrace them as equals. Furthermore, *The Course* encourages us to take the first step—the most difficult step—to extend our hand and heart to those who have asked for forgiveness and want to make amends for their mistakes. This is at the core of what the second tenet of the Third Sacred Question teaches.

Next, I began to focus on the third tenet of the Third Sacred Question. I interpreted the third tenet as a call to action: *What have you done today to contribute to a better tomorrow?* It occurred to me as I thought about the third tenet that what was expected of me was something significant because I had been blessed with certain talents and ability. I was capable of doing more. I just wasn't sure *what* that something was.

CHAPTER 24

Birds and Roses

One of *The Course* assignments is to observe birds as they feed. This required me to research bird feeders and purchase one. I visited Wild Birds Unlimited in Carlsbad, California and bought a rustic log cabin, all-wood box-styled Cedar Feeder Hopper made by Garden that was fully assembled and had more detail on it than a Rembrandt painting. I also purchased a Garden hummingbird feeder because the salesperson told me I would enjoy watching hummingbirds feed. He was right! My purchase was made complete with various sunflower seeds the salesperson recommended for my new box-styled feeder.

Another assignment was to study roses, so the next day, I drove to Corona Del Mar to Roger's Gardens, one of Southern California's premier flower and landscaping stores. I wanted to attend a lecture by Mr. Miller, an expert on roses from Weeks' Roses of Wasco, California, one of the largest commercial rose growers in the United States. Mr. Miller talked about how to feed and prune roses during the winter months. The amphitheater at Roger's Garden was crowded. Attendees represented yet another subculture of millions of people who could be dubbed "rose enthusiasts." Earlier I conducted a search for "roses" on the Internet and found 110 million entries so I wasn't surprised by the diverse crowd and their level of interest in roses. I sat in the rear and listened for 30 minutes as Mr. Miller talked about his passion for roses and shared his expertise on how to prune and care for these beautiful flowers in the winter. Thus began my formal education on roses.

On a separate visit to the San Diego Botanical Gardens in Encinitas, a horticulturist explained to me that much of the soil in San Diego was either very sandy or heavy clay. These types of soils benefit from the addition of organic material. He told me when planting roses I should mix the soil with compost, composted bark and some composted manure. I winced at the thought of having to perform that putrid task!

I also contacted the Pacific Southwest Chapter of the American Rose Society to obtain information on the types and varieties of roses. I learned there are more than 2,600 certified Consulting Rosarians, or CR as they are known professionally, who contribute their time and talents to educate people on roses and the rose culture. It was in my discussions with a CR that I learned there are 70,000 registered roses, each having its own name and unique attributes.

Another Rosarian told me about the symbolism and meaning of roses. For example, red roses convey love, respect and passion. Now, I understood why the symbol for *The Course* was a red rose.

Pink roses symbolize grace and gentility and are considered the rose of sweet thoughts. Yellow roses signify friendship, joy, gladness and freedom as well as the promise of a new beginning. White roses are the color of spiritual love and purity and are often called the Bridal Rose. Lavender roses represent love at first sight and enchantment, while orange roses are associated with passionate desire, pure enthusiasm and fascination.

Another interesting thing I learned about roses was the symbolism associated with the number of roses someone receives. A single rose symbolizes love at first sight while two roses convey mutual love. Three roses tells the recipient "I love you" while a dozen roses is asking you to "go steady." If someone sends you 108 roses, it is a marriage proposal while 999 roses symbolize eternal and everlasting love. When I asked the CR what 1,000 roses symbolizes she replied jokingly, "It means you own a flower shop!" I had a good laugh over that one.

Ajay also suggested I buy a book on birds so I could identify the various kinds of birds that visited my feeder. I decided on the National Audubon Society's *Field Guide to Birds, Western Region (North America)* edition by Miklos D. F. Udvardy and John Ferrand, Jr. (published in 2000 by Alfred A. Knopf, New York). For $20 I had my bird Bible complete with 676 full-color photographs of birds!

For the next two weeks, I sat at my kitchen table at various times of the day looking out the window to watch the birds on the feeders. During my observations, I noticed how larger birds intimidated smaller birds. I also noticed that larger birds like the Western Scrub-Jays made a mess on the bird feeders by knocking a good amount of seed onto the ground in order to retrieve their preferred sunflower seeds and other favorite ingredients in the mix. Ironically, this selective process of picking and choosing their favorite seeds made it easier for the smaller birds and squirrels to feed on the ground. From time to time, there were a few squabbles over the discarded seed. The Western Scrub-Jays wanted all of it! They squawked and flapped their wings to discourage the sparrows and mourning doves from eating the spilled seed on the ground.

I also observed that most of the birds arrived in pairs and one bird would snack while their partner stood guard. Then, they would swap roles. When they had their fill, they flew away. The hummingbirds were especially interesting. It appeared they danced and played as they took turns at the four-flowered hummingbird feeder. Legend suggests that hummingbirds float free of time carrying our hopes for love, a sense of joy and the celebration of life. As I watched these marvelous, miniature creatures perform outside my kitchen window, I was reminded of an old saying that goes, "a hummingbird's delicate grace reminds us that life is rich, beauty is everywhere, every personal connection has meaning and that laughter is life's sweetest creation."

As I watched the birds perform their various rituals while feeding, my mind was relaxed and calm. No other thoughts interrupted me. I was mesmerized by the movements and behavioral patterns of the birds. I experienced a sense of peace and satisfaction by watching the birds on the feeders. I was not haunted by any demons or distracted by other thoughts. It was just as Ajay had told me it would be when he described his experiences with birds during our conversation at Horseshoe Bay. The only thing Ajay didn't tell me was how to keep those pesky squirrels off my bird feeders!

There are many lessons we can apply to the power of the Divine Source by observing nature because we are part of it! One of the most powerful lessons you will take away from these exercises is the importance of loving all things, great and small, in this world. While most species are capable of displaying affection, only human beings are capable of love on an emotional and intellectual level. As we grow older, our capacity for love increases. It is magnified in so many simple ways. For example, bending down to move the snail off the sidewalk rather than squashing it is a small act of love. Holding the door open for the person behind you is an act of civility as well as love and kindness. Allowing the other person to finish their sentence or thought without interrupting is an act of courtesy, but also love and respect.

Throughout life, we experience different types of love—emotional and intellectual love. For example, there's a type of love you would give to your spouse or partner beyond just fulfilling their sexual desires; the kind

10,000 Days

of love we give and receive from our family and friends when we celebrate special occasions; and, the kind of love and joy we give and receive from experiencing life's special moments every day. Certainly, this includes learning to love life and respecting the wonders of nature.

The Course reminds us that people experience love in one of three forms. The Greeks interpreted the three forms of love through their mythology. Eros, the god of sexual desires, is the most basic and physical form of love. It is the one we are most familiar with because it is symbolized by the eroticism of physical contact between people. Agape is a spiritual love we display for a neighbor or friend. Ironically, the Greeks consider Eros and Agape to be *impersonal* loves. Amor is considered the validation of the human experience because it is the only *personal* love of the three types. Amor is the romantic love that requires courage on the part of one person to feel a deep sense of love for another human being; and, that can only come from the heart.

Another reason why *The Course* includes the bird feeder exercise is to help us calm our mind and find peace within. Serenity scares away our demons. The most difficult part of changing human behavior is quieting the mind and simply relaxing. Ajay reminded me that too often we're running at full speed—burning the candle at both ends or clicking on all twelve cylinders. When we're up against a deadline that level of intensity can be explained. But, eventually it causes physical exhaustion and mental burnout. Only when we relax and calm our mind, can we begin to appreciate those things we take for granted like the air we breathe, the green forests and the blue oceans. In other words, the wonderful creations of the Divine Source are there for our enjoyment, so enjoy!

When we slow down and observe nature as a part of our being rather than an extension of where we live, we move closer to living a life worth remembering. It's the difference between walking along the shore and swimming in the ocean! *The Course* is trying to help us *experience* life and live it to the fullest. The only way we can accomplish that is to expand our capacity to love. Although the process is actually quite simple, it is difficult for most people to slow down long enough to stop and smell the roses—literally!

These exercises will not only help you calm your mind, but they are designed to help you increase your capacity to give and receive love. Also, these exercises will help prepare you for The Kingdom of Roses where you will develop your relationship with the Divine Source. It is through the Divine Source that all things are possible including the magnificent experience of divineness.

Once you learn how to cultivate a spiritually-based love for all living things, you will be ready to enter The Kingdom of Roses, discover your higher purpose and possibly experience your divineness.

CHAPTER 25

The Kingdom of Roses

*T*he *Course* defines The Kingdom of Roses as a spiritual temple within each of us where the Divine Source dwells and our Inner Spirit flourishes. Here is a passage from Dr. Kavi's book that describes this sacred temple within us:

It is that sacred place within each of us where the essence of our life and our sense of purpose cannot be challenged or suppressed by the ego.

It is the place where physical and spiritual balance meet so that we might live in harmony and truth.

It is the place where your heart speaks the language of compassion and love.

It is the place where our Inner Spirit blossoms and love supersedes all other emotions and responses.

It is the place where we count our joys before our problems and troubles.

It is the place where our outer appearance is a reflection of our inner peace.

It is the place where our Inner Spirit is nurtured from within and we have no wants or needs except to share our unique gift of love with others.

It is the place where we exist in a state of grace with the Divine Source because we have found purpose, peace and passion in our life.

It is the place where life is complete and whole.

It is the place where we transcend our humanness by recognizing the Divine Source permeates us through love.

CHAPTER 26

The Dublin Conversation

T he week before I was scheduled to leave for Ireland, Ajay called to invite me to travel with him and his executive team on their new BBJ-3 corporate jet. Ajay told me TGC was bringing seven executives to the World Congress of International Corporations in Dublin and since I was speaking there, and I knew many of his colleagues, they wanted me to join them. It was a thoughtful gesture and I accepted on the spot.

On Friday evening, I drove from San Diego to Newport Beach. The 90-mile drive was surprisingly quick. The air was cool and the November skies were crystal clear. Ajay had reserved a room for me at the Fairmont Hotel in Newport Beach. I arrived at 7:15 pm ready for a relaxing massage at their Willow Stream Spa and a light dinner in the hotel restaurant. The five-star service was fabulous. The next morning, Ajay met me for breakfast where we talked about the upcoming conference in Dublin and my assignments for *The Course*. Afterwards, we drove the short distance to the corporate terminal at John Wayne Orange County Airport for our non-stop flight to Republic Airport located in Farmingdale, New York.

This is where Bob Tohmy, TGC's chief executive officer, and Lin Yao, TGC's senior vice president of marketing, would join us for the flight to Dublin. We were scheduled to arrive in Dublin about 6:30 am on Saturday morning following our overnight flight.

Once aboard the corporate BBJ-3, Ajay re-introduced me to his TGC colleagues. Although I had met most of them before, it had been nearly two years since we had last worked together on their business excellence initiative. It only took a few minutes to break the ice and feel among friends once again. Then Ajay gave me a tour of their new corporate aircraft which had been delivered four months earlier. It was the largest of three jets TGC leased and was well-suited for international flights. The jet's main cabin was outfitted with ten large business-class sleeper seats that stretched six feet long and measured 32 inches wide. Behind the main cabin section was a deluxe lounge and dining galley that extended over the wings. In the rear of the plane was the CEO's private conference area complete with four lounge chairs, a desk and a separate suite with a double bed, bathroom and shower. The jet was also equipped with a treadmill and exercise cycle to keep passengers fit. Ajay could tell from my facial expressions as we toured the plane that I was impressed. "Wow, this is the way to travel," I commented. "No security lines, no screaming kids and no flight delays on the tarmac!"

Since Ajay was the senior TGC executive aboard the jet, he occupied the executive suite. After thirty minutes of conducting business with his management team, Ajay adjourned their meeting and invited me to sit with him in the private suite conference area where we sipped champagne and ate a healthy breakfast consisting of fresh fruit, juice and cooked-to-order omelets. The flight attendant refilled our champagne glasses and then Ajay requested two cups of green tea for us. A few minutes later, the flight attendant arrived with a pot of boiling water. I was enjoying the superior service!

During breakfast, we talked about business challenges facing TGC and its competitors as well as ideas on how to grow their industry. We also reviewed each other's presentation notes for the Dublin leadership conference. Afterwards, Ajay asked me to update him on my *Course* assignments that included observing birds, researching roses and performing the BAG It exercise. I began by sharing with him my BAG It exercise and reciting my list of blessings, accomplishments and goals which I had recorded daily in my journal. Ajay complimented me for being disciplined and performing this daily ritual over the past few weeks.

Then, we discussed the significance of roses and their relationship to *The Course.* Ajay explained the history, symbolism and attributes of roses. According to Greek mythology, the rose was the flower that gave life to a beautiful nymph and became a significant part of Greek culture. In Hindu legend, upon seeing the beauty of a rose, Brahma created a bride for Vishnu. In England, the heraldic Tudor Rose became the emblem of British royalty. Confucius wrote about roses in 500 BC when he found them growing in the Imperial Rose Garden of the Chinese Emperor. Confucius also noted that fossil evidence revealed the rose had existed for nearly 40 million years. Ajay also told me that modern roses were discovered in Persia around 1700 BC and over the centuries, roses came to symbolize everything from love to jealousy and death to rebirth.

Ajay told me the relevance of the rose to *The Course of 10,000 Days*® is based on several factors. First, the rose was dedicated by the Greeks to the Goddess of Love and Beauty, Aphrodite. The rose is the greatest symbol and expression of love; and, love is at the core of *The Course's* teachings because love is our greatest gift. Secondly, the rose represents the eternal mystery—the continuity of life—and through the symbolism of the rose, *The Course* encourages people to resurrect their Inner Spirit and rejuvenate their lives by finding the gentle balance between their ego and Inner Spirit. This is how the rose came to be a symbol of mystery and secrecy. "Mystery glows in the rose bed; the secret is hidden in the rose," wrote the Persian poet, Farid ud-din Attar in the 12th century.

The rose is also the symbol of *confidentiality* dating back to the Greeks who held private meetings in temple rooms where the decorative ceilings were painted with roses. This was the origin of the Latin phrase *sub rosa* (under the roses) which symbolizes confidentiality. Ajay reminded me that everything I shared with him as my *Course* counselor was held in Sub Rosa—the strictest confidence.

There is some debate among flower experts as to what constitutes the *perfect rose*. J. E. Cirlot, the author of Pablo Picasso's biography, believed that the *meaning* of roses is symbolized by its number of layers of petals and colors. In my research, I discovered *A Book About Roses* written by Samuel Reynolds Hole in 1896. Hole served as president of the National Rose Society and he defined the perfect rose in similar terms as Cirlot. Dr. Kavi believes that a rose with seven layers of petals constitutes the perfect rose.

More importantly, *The Course of 10,000 Days*® uses the power and symbolism of the rose to remind people that life is a journey of discovery and transformation. And the ultimate transformation we seek is to achieve a state of inner peace and life balance between our physical self and Inner Spirit. *The Course* refers to this spiritual state as The Kingdom of Roses. Once we enter The Kingdom of Roses, our challenge is to master seven virtues. Each virtue is linked to one of the seven layers of petals of the rose. Only when you have mastered the seven layers of petals can you fully experience The Kingdom of Roses.

At that point in our airborne conversation, Ajay retrieved two beautiful roses—one white and one red—that were sitting in a vase on the counter behind him. He pulled the white rose from the vase and said to me, "During *The Course* retreat, one of the exercises Dr. Kavi has us perform is to smell a freshly cut rose to heighten our senses."

Ajay handed the white rose to me and said, "*The Course* teaches us that the fragrance of a rose is an important feature that relaxes people and calms their ego. It even acts as an aphrodisiac for some people. Dr. Kavi studied roses in depth and found that a rose's fragrance is the secret substance that embodies its true nature."

Jean-Paul Sartre once described the spiritual essence of scent as "a vaporized body which has remained completely itself, but which has become a volatile spirit." Perhaps Sartre also was describing the scent of the rose.

David Austin said, "Scent is the soul of the rose. It is something that we cannot hold in our hands; it is always shifting and changing."

Ajay put the white rose back in the vase and retrieved the red rose for me to examine. He delicately held it in his hand and gently began peeling back the petals as he counted them. It had seven layers of petals—the perfect rose!

Ajay said, "In his writings, J.E. Cirlot described the seven-layered rose as very rare and special. Cirlot believed that the perfect rose refers to the seven directions of space, the seven planets and the seven degrees of perfection. It is in this context, Cirlot believed, that the perfect rose appears in the emblem DCCXXIII of the 1702 painting *Ars Symbolica* by Bosch and in the 1629 book *Summum Bonum* by Robert Fludd. In the *Ars Symbolica* there is an interesting link to birds which is why Dr. Kavi gave us the bird feeder assignment. He wanted us to discover the link between birds, roses and our divineness."

Reaching into his weather-worn, brown leather saddle bag, Ajay took out an art book and opened it to a marked page. He showed me a picture and said, "Look here, Tom, the 84th emblem of the *Ars Symbolica* refers to the peacock's tail and the blending together of all its colors. According to the *Ars Symbolica*, this symbolizes totality. Its relationship to *The Course* is this: as we live our lives, we are trying to merge the colors of our life experiences into one cohesive theme in order to achieve perfection. Just as the peacock can merge all its feathers into a single visual image, it can also spread its tail widely to display its array of beautiful feathers and demonstrate their individuality, vitality and uniqueness.

"At *The Course* retreat, Dr. Kavi explained why the rose was such an important symbol. He told us, 'Roses are the messengers of our deepest and most sacred feelings. Roses have a language of their own. As gifts, roses are capable of expressing all shades of feelings and passions. And like people, the rose has endured as a metaphor through centuries—including surviving a ban for at least 11 centuries in Western civilization by the Catholic Church.'"

Ajay put the red rose back in the vase and reached into his saddle bag once again to pull out a journal that looked exactly like *The Course* journal he had given me at Lake Tahoe. He opened it to a passage on roses which he had carefully marked with a dried rose petal.

"Here's how Dr. Kavi summarized Cirlot's description of the rose," Ajay said as he read from his journal:

The single rose is a symbol of completion, of consummate achievement and perfection. The ideas associated with these qualities include the mystic Centre, the heart, the garden of Eros, the paradise of Dante, the Beloved Master, and the emblem of Venus. Other symbolic meanings are derived from the color of roses and the number of its petals. The white rose symbolizes purity. The blue rose is symbolic of the impossible. The golden rose is a symbol of absolute achievement; and the red rose symbolizes love. When the rose is round in shape, it corresponds to the Mandala. The seven-petalled rose alludes to the septenary pattern—that is, the seven directions of space, the seven planets, the seven degrees of perfection—and symbolizes perfection. Thus, the seven layers of petals of a rose represent perfection. The eight-petalled rose symbolizes regeneration.

Ajay continued to share his knowledge on the rose—how it encompassed the history of both eastern and western civilization as well as the power of its mythology. He also described how the rose was prized for thousands of years by many cultures and has come to symbolize so many different things for our generation. Today, the rose is associated with mythology, religion, art, literature and, most significantly, romance.

Ajay then placed the rose vase on the desk between us and picking up the white rose once more, he said, "It was James Matthew Barrie, the creator of Peter Pan, who told a graduating class at St. Andrews University on May 3, 1922 that 'God made memories so that we could have roses in December.'"

I smiled acknowledging Ajay's mastery of such timely quotes and glanced at the white rose that sat on the desk between us.

"Let me tell you about The Kingdom of Roses and its relationship to *The Course of 10,000 Days*®," Ajay said. "This white rose symbolizes purity and life. And as you can see here, this rose has eight layers of petals."

"Rejuvenation," I exclaimed!

"Yes, exactly," Ajay replied. "What you see here are two beautiful roses—one represents perfection, the other represents rejuvenation," Ajay continued. "This red rose is among the rarest in the world because it has seven layers which is considered by many to represent the perfect rose. The perfect rose reminds us that we are capable of divineness in this life because the Divine Source made us in its perfect image and likeness. But to achieve divineness we must rejuvenate ourselves and master the seven virtues upon entering The Kingdom of Roses. And each of the seven virtues is represented by a separate layer of petals from this perfect red rose."

With that explanation, Ajay briefly described each of the seven virtues symbolized by the seven layers of petals—for they hold the key to discovering our higher purpose in life. Ajay held the seven-layered red rose in his hand and began to gently peel back each layer as he described the seven virtues symbolized by the perfect rose.

"The first layer of petals," Ajay said, "represents Humility. Humility is the second most beautiful word in the English language because its very definition suggests we have placed the Divine Source and the interest of others before ourselves. Humility requires us to acknowledge there is a universal power greater than any of us, individually or collectively. Humility is also the second greatest of all virtues because it implies a willingness to sacrifice our time, talents and even our life for others. Humility suppresses pride. It inhibits us from being judgmental and critical of others because through humility we are aware of our own imperfections. Humility also keeps us from getting angry or seeking revenge because we understand what it means to be less than perfect."

Ajay continued. "The second layer of petals symbolizes the virtue of Compassion. Compassion requires us to be both tolerant and forgiving. Tolerance demands that we learn patience and withhold judgment. Too often, we rush to judgment based on our first emotion and ignore the facts. *The Course* teaches us to calm our mind in order to quell our desire for revenge which we seek in moments of anger.

"Forgiveness is the most difficult component of Compassion because it requires us to let go of revenge and release the anger trapped in our heart. It is very difficult to forgive someone when your ego has been wounded and negative emotions scar your memory. Compassion also requires us to accept people as they are in the moment. This level of acceptance is difficult because we are manipulated by our ego which wants to change the world to suit the ego's selfish needs. So, we attempt to change people by trying to undo certain undesirable things about them—their personality and appearance, their likes and dislikes, their prejudices and biases, their thoughts, behaviors, beliefs and feelings. But, this is an exercise in futility because people cannot be changed by others. People can only change themselves. The secret to being compassionate is to discover patience and open your heart to forgive people who offend you. It is by our positive and compassionate example that others find their way.

"The third layer of petals," Ajay noted, "represents the virtue of Selflessness. *The Course* reminds us that by giving of our time and talent to others we perform one of the greatest expressions of love a person can bestow. People who perform acts of kindness are following in the footsteps of the greatest teachers. Before we can enter The Kingdom of Roses, we must serve others. We must feed the hungry, minister to those less fortunate and care for the sick."

Ajay gently peeled back another layer of petals and told me, "The fourth layer of petals symbolizes Generosity. People who are generous know generosity is more of a gift from the heart than a contribution from their wallet. It was Albert Camus who said, 'Too many have dispensed with generosity in order to practice charity.'

"Generosity should not be confused with charity, philanthropy or with donating clothes and money to help others in need. Generosity is much different. It is organic in the sense that it is an individual act usually performed spontaneously and randomly without seeking credit or praise for such actions. Generosity can take the form of a kind word to someone who is upset. It is holding the door open for your elders or performing a kind deed for someone who will never know you did it but will appreciate the thought and be touched by your kindness and loving action. With regard to Generosity, Dr. Kavi taught us a beautiful poem by John Wesley. Let me read it to you. I think that says it better than anything else I can tell you about Generosity."

> *Do all the good you can,*
> *By all the means you can,*
> *In all the ways you can,*
> *In all the places you can,*
> *At all the times you can,*
> *To all the people you can,*
> *As long as ever you can.*

I reflected on the words of John Wesley as Ajay peeled back the fifth layer of petals. "The fifth layer of rose petals represents Justice," Ajay said. "Before we can enter The Kingdom of Roses we must embrace the true meaning of Justice. When *The Course* talks about Justice, it does not mean we should apply a legal definition or judicial standard that is limited by the laws of society. Too often, justice is confused with judgment. What is fair? What is the appropriate punishment for a thief or murderer? That is not Justice. That is revenge disguised as justice to appease the ego needs of a vengeful society. It is what constitutes law and order in any society. And while it is necessary, it should not be mistaken for Justice.

"Justice requires us to develop an understanding of others no matter how despicable those persons might be. It is Compassion and tolerance and doing the ethical thing even when the mob is shouting you down. In this sense, Justice includes providing education and healthcare for all because an ignorant and unhealthy population is an indictment against society. It is feeding the hungry and sheltering the homeless. This is Justice.

"Alexander Solzhenitsyn, the great Russian writer and thought leader who was imprisoned for many years because he had the courage to express his views against the communist Soviet state, said, 'Justice is conscience, not a personal conscience but the conscience of the whole of humanity. Those who clearly recognize the voice of their own conscience usually recognize also the voice of justice.'

"Justice is also the search for truth and living your truth. Galileo Galilei said, 'All truths are easy to understand once they are discovered; the point is to discover them.'"

Ajay added, "I always thought Steve Jobs, the talented founder of Apple, had a wonderful perspective on living one's truth when he said, 'Your time is limited so don't waste it living someone else's life. Don't be trapped by dogma which is living with the results of other people's thinking. Don't let the noise of others' opinions drown out your inner voice. And, most importantly, have the courage to follow your heart and intuition. They somehow already know what you truly want to become. Everything else is secondary.'"

As Ajay spoke, I recalled the words of the former slave, Frederick Douglass, who said, "Where justice is denied, where poverty is enforced, where ignorance prevails and where any one class is made to feel that society is an organized conspiracy to oppress, rob and degrade them, neither persons nor their property will be safe."

Ajay continued his explanation of the seven petals. "In a democratic society and inclusive political environment, Fairness is very much a part of Justice. However, from the perspective of *The Course*, it is important to separate the two because as the German philosopher Immanuel Kant believed, 'Fairness is contingent upon the hearts of those who enforce the moral law. And sometimes the moral law is at odds with what is fair. When this happens, Fairness is suppressed for political purposes. Wrongs are perpetrated by people who think they are acting on behalf of what is morally right when, in fact, they are abusing the standard of fairness and compromising justice.' I suppose this explains how Joan of Arc was burned at the stake or Japanese-American citizens were marched off to internment camps at the outset of World War II."

Ajay reflected on his own words for a moment and then added, "Having said that, however, the extent to which a society or person is *fair* depends on how much love is in their hearts. Someone who is filled with love does not seek revenge or harshly judge another person without first having done everything that meets the definition of Fairness."

Ajay then spoke to me about Peace. "The sixth layer of the perfect rose represents Peace. *The Course* defines Peace as that state where we live in harmony with the Divine Source. In this state, we are one with our Inner Spirit. There is a profound sense of calm and order in our life. We have no extreme wants. We do not covet what others possess. When our life is orderly we are tranquil and un-needy. Everything we truly require is within us. Our dreams are within reach because we believe in ourselves and know all is possible. Love abounds and permeates our senses with a relaxed, soothing contentment. While material things are to be enjoyed, we are not consumed with the pursuit of those things that only offer us a false sense of security and temporary comfort.

"Peace begins with each of us. If we desire Peace in the world, we must first practice Peace in our own hearts. Our thoughts must be peaceful and not filled with spite, revenge or hostility towards others. As a nation, we cannot covet the natural resources of another country whether it is oil, gas, precious metals or water. We cannot covet territory or the lifestyle others enjoy. Peace requires us to accept people for their positive attributes as well as their imperfections. Peace also requires us to be still and listen to our Inner Spirit.

"*The Course* teaches us that our Inner Spirit will send us clear messages when we pray or seek its direction or counsel," Ajay told me. "Listening requires courage and strength. We must have the courage to listen for new possibilities in our life and the strength to quiet the ego so we can recognize those new possibilities and opportunities when they come to us, especially when they come to us disguised as something we don't expect!"

Ajay then offered an interesting example. "Dr. Kavi once asked me, 'Do you believe in angels?' Frankly, I wasn't really sure if I believed in angels. I had to think about it for a while because as a child my mind was filled with all sorts of notions about God, heaven, angels and demons. But as I matured, I discounted many of those religious images and symbols for lack of scientific proof. I told Dr. Kavi this and he said to me, 'Ajay, do you think we are in this world alone? Do you really believe that the Divine Source would place us here, stranded, without direction, or the spiritual

10,000 Days

resources we need to achieve our divineness?

Of course not! Frequently, angels are sent to help us choose our path in life. Perhaps, it's meeting that special someone at the airport or department store and we marry them. Perhaps, an angel comes to us in the form of a friend who tells us about a new job or financial opportunity. Perhaps, that angel comes to us in the form of a stranger on the subway who offers us a word of inspiration or hope after a difficult day at work. This is the Divine Source's way of interceding on our behalf and trying to help us fulfill our destiny and achieve our higher purpose in life. Everything is connected and everyone on earth is connected to each other. Angels are part of the Divine Source's universal support system that connects us to each other.'"

Ajay added, "Although faith is universal, each of us must find our own path to our Inner Spirit. Some of us choose a formal religion while others search for life's purpose through another truth which is greater than ourselves. But in the final analysis, our Inner Spirit will guide us to that higher place. This is why Peace is the choice of wise people."

Ajay stretched out his arm and handed me the perfect rose. As he stood up in the spacious cabin of BBJ-3 jet to circulate the blood in his legs, he said to me, "Do you know what the seventh layer of the perfect rose represents?"

I thought for a moment but realized it was a rhetorical question as Ajay sat down and said to me, "The seventh layer of the perfect rose represents Grace."

I smiled acknowledging both the simplicity of the answer and its obvious selection. Ajay then described Grace and its relevance to The Kingdom of Roses. "*The Course* teaches us there are two types of Grace. The first type is intrinsic Grace. This type of Grace is realized by very few people. Unfortunately, not everyone manifests intrinsic Grace although we all have the potential to do so.

"When I look at my wife," Ajay said, "I see in her that elusive, but beautiful, attribute we call intrinsic Grace. It is very difficult to describe in words. Yet, when someone possesses intrinsic Grace you know it by their calm demeanor. You see it in their patient and quiet ways. Their words are soothing. They are non-judgmental. There is an inherent goodness about people who possess intrinsic Grace. They make the very best friends because they only desire what is best for you. And yet, when you want their feedback or insight, they will give it to you in honest, but nurturing, words.

"The second type of Grace is Divine Grace. It comes to us from the Divine Source through our Inner Spirit. Divine Grace is the primary source of our inspiration and internal guidance. It is the influence of the Divine Source operating in each of us to regenerate and strengthen our goodness. Divine Grace comes to us often so we can cope with life's challenges, difficult people and all the frustrating situations we encounter every day—from traffic jams to workplace problems. When we slow down long enough to hear the voice of our Inner Spirit we can experience that state of Divine Grace that inspires us to do the right thing instead of acting out our negative emotions. Now, you can see why it is so important to allow your Inner Spirit to be rejuvenated."

I asked Ajay, "Is Divine Grace an extension of prayer?"

"No," Ajay replied. "But, Divine Grace comes to us as the result of prayer or meditation. We receive Divine Grace when we ask the Divine Source to intervene in our life. Again, in order to connect with the Divine Source, we must make that spiritual connection through our Inner Spirit. All meaningful requests made to the Divine Source come not from our human dimension, but rather, our spiritual dimension. This is one more reason why it is important for us to have a relationship with our Inner Spirit. This is why *The Course* believes in a balanced life in which our ego and Inner Spirit act in harmony instead of competing for our thoughts, emotions, actions and time.

"If we closely examine the attributes of love, kindness, service, a willingness to care for others and mercy, you will realize that our ego defines them quite differently than does our Inner Spirit. This is why existing in a state of Grace is important if you want to live what *The Course* teaches. Let me give you an example of each attribute. Love—or should I say true love—takes time. This is the domain of our Inner Spirit. But, pleasurable love in the form of infatuation and sexual desires is the domain of our ego. Kindness, justice, mercy and service to others are the domain of our Inner Spirit. Charity is the purview of our ego. Forgiveness can only be practiced by our Inner Spirit, whereas pardoning someone for their wrongs is the work of our ego.

"Also, remember that the only way you can put the seven petals to work in your life is through your Inner Spirit. Unfortunately, the ego is not fully capable of Humility, Compassion, Selflessness, Generosity, Justice, Peace and Grace. Only your Inner Spirit can summon and practice these seven virtues. All the great metaphysical teachers understand this fact. This is why we are constantly challenged to grow beyond our selfish interests and seek our higher purpose in life. This is why The Kingdom of Roses exists for us. Now, you see how Grace is the glue that binds together the other six layers of petals of the perfect rose."

As Ajay placed the seven-layered rose he was holding back in its vase, he commented, "I think it was Archbishop Fulton Sheen who once said, 'Anyone can love a rose, but it takes a great heart to love a leaf!'"

I smiled at Ajay's timely quip as he placed the red rose in the vase without disturbing the leaves surrounding the rose's stem. Ajay stood up once again to stretch his legs and invited me to rest for the remainder of our flight. We had spent several hours talking about the symbolism and power of the rose and its seven virtues. He had given me much to think about as our airplane approached Long Island's Republic Airport.

Our stop-over at Republic Airport lasted 50 minutes—just long enough to pick up Bob Tohmy and Lin Yao and stretch our legs while the corporate BBJ-3 was refueled and serviced for our trans-Atlantic flight to Dublin Airport. The November weather on Long Island was sunny, but cold, with temperatures measuring a brisk 42 degrees. Ajay said it was "good preparation for the Irish weather that awaited us!"

As we waited, I quickly got re-acquainted with Bob Tohmy and met Lin Yao, who had joined TGC a year ago. Lin was born and raised near Beijing, educated at UC Berkeley and clearly understood the marketing and growth opportunities for TGC's products in Asia. We chatted in the executive terminal about Bob's goals for the conference in Dublin and our favorite golf courses in Ireland. Royal County Down in Newcastle, some 90 miles north of Dublin, got the most votes. We also talked about some of the tourist sites we planned to visit while in Dublin.

We all agreed that a visit to Johnnie Fox's pub, located in Glencullen atop the Dublin Mountains, was a priority during our visit. Bob Tohmy, whose grandparents were born in County Cork, told us that Hooley Night was the best time to visit Johnnie Fox's. Just as Bob was about to explain Hooley Night to us, our flight attendant politely interrupted and requested that we re-board the jet. No sooner had we taken our seats and fastened our seatbelts than we were roaring down Runway 32 at Republic Airport enroute to Dublin.

At 6:15 am, we touched down in the capital of the Emerald Isle. It was the most enjoyable flight I have ever taken. The food and onboard service were exceptional and everyone enjoyed at least three hours of peaceful rest in our sleeper business-class seats. I also took time to think about the seven petals of the rose which Ajay revealed and reflect on how to apply them in my life.

Gray November skies greeted our early morning arrival as we descended over the west coast of Ireland. Clouds covered much of the Aran Islands which lie twenty miles off the rugged west coast of Ireland. It was apparent that the powerful waves and winds stirred by the Atlantic

Ocean had hammered and re-shaped this beautiful coastline over millions of years. As we crossed over Galway, the gray skies gave way to a beautiful sunrise and revealed that region's growing cityscape. Below us, the towns of Athlone and Maynooth were painted in lush green farmlands, beautiful lakes and crystal blue rivers. It was almost 6:30 am on Saturday morning and the serene Irish countryside was tranquil and sleepy.

Our landing approach took us east over the Irish Sea for ten miles before turning back into the headwinds to make our final approach at Dublin Airport. Crossing over land once again, I could see the brown, dormant fairways of Portmarnock Golf Course awaiting a herd of anxious weekend golfers who were determined to brave the November chill and crosswinds to play its popular links.

A few minutes later, we touched down and taxied to the executive terminal. There, we retrieved our luggage, quickly cleared Irish customs and boarded a spacious travel coach to make the 30-minute trip to downtown Dublin and the Four Seasons Hotel where we were staying. After checking-in, we took advantage of the only down time in our schedule and got some much-needed sleep before our afternoon tour of Dublin began.

We met in the hotel lobby at 2:00 pm and boarded our private coach for an afternoon guided tour of Dublin. We visited several sites including Dublin Castle, Trinity College, which houses the famous Book of Kells, Kilmainham Gaol, Ireland's most famous prison where leaders of the 1916 Rebellion were executed and, of course, the Guinness Storehouse where 250 years of Guinness history are on display. The revolving bar that sits atop the Guinness factory provided a spectacular view of Dublin city and a fitting end to our tour as we drank our Guinness Extra Stout. Afterwards, we assembled at the Shelbourne Hotel's renowned Horseshoe Bar for cocktails. Bob Tohmy insisted we each sample a shot of two popular Irish whiskeys, Middleton Rare and Jameson 1780. I was glad I did not have to pay that bar tab!

Braving the wind-whipped November night, we strolled down the street past St. Stephen's Green to the beautiful Merrion Hotel for dinner at The Restaurant Patrick Guilbaud. The wonderful food and service left no doubt that this was the best restaurant in Dublin. After dinner, we walked through Temple Bar where we enjoyed the local music and sampled some of Dublin's best known beers as well as coffee to stay warm. By 11:00 pm we were back at the Four Seasons Dublin and ready for a good night's sleep.

On Sunday, the weather was beautiful. We ate an early breakfast and made the two-hour trip to Newcastle, Northern Ireland where we played the Royal County Down Golf Course. The temperamental Irish weather cooperated with sunny skies and temperatures in the low 50s. It was one of the most beautiful but demanding golf courses I had ever played. My high score reflected the challenge! But, as Ajay reminded me, exploring Ireland's famous golf courses and seeing its spectacular countryside was not only part of being a good tourist, it was also good therapy according to *The Course of 10,000 Days®*.

We returned to Dublin at 4:00 pm in time to change and attend the opening conference ceremonies at the Dublin Convention Center that evening. It was a short ride from the Four Seasons Hotel to the convention center where we joined nearly 2,000 leaders from 38 countries for the opening general session and the international reception. Diageo PLC hosted the event which surpassed everyone's expectations!

On Monday, Ajay and I delivered our speeches. Both presentations were well received and we both enjoyed standing-room-only crowds. It was nice to get my speech behind me on the first day of the conference so I could relax and enjoy the other sessions and speakers on Tuesday and Wednesday. I spent my evenings with Bob Tohmy, Ajay and the rest of the

TGC entourage entertaining customers at Dublin's popular pubs and theatres. We also experienced Hooley Night at Johnnie Fox's in Glencullen.

When the conference adjourned, I had planned to spend my two free days researching my family roots in County Wexford and County Mayo while the TGC team met with international clients and toured TGC's plant operations in Dublin, Cork and Belfast. During a previous discussion on *The Course*, Ajay had talked to me about the importance of understanding *who* you are and *where* you came from.

"Part of your legacy," he told me, "is not only knowing your family roots and genealogy, but equally important, it's knowing your cultural DNA. In other words, do you know how you arrived at this point in your life? In the context of *The Course*, each of us has been selected to live at this precise time and moment in history. Why? What are the gifts you bring to this era? Why are *you* here and not someone else in your place? Your existence is not a mistake. There are reasons why you are living in this moment." Ajay's statement intrigued me. It prompted me to seek answers to those questions during this visit so I could place my family roots and genealogy in the proper context.

I also wanted to take some time to learn about the Irish culture and how the Irish overcame 500 years of political struggle and repression, religious persecution, the Great Famine of 1845-1852, the mass exodus of a generation to America in the early 1900s and, most recently, The Troubles—as the 30-year period of violence and bloodshed is referred to—which crippled Northern Ireland from 1968 to 1998.

The late American novelist Leon Uris referred to Northern Ireland as a "terrible beauty." Fortunately, as a result of the Good Friday Agreement that was signed in 1998 by the Catholics and Protestant leaders, Northern Ireland is safe to travel and visit. We could attest to that fact since we had a wonderful time visiting the hospitable town of Newcastle in Northern Ireland where Royal County Down Golf Course is located. Most important, the fragile peace is giving economic hope to a new generation by providing an environment where people of all faiths can safely live, work and raise their families.

CHAPTER 27

Peace

Following the closing session of the conference, Ajay and I walked through St. Stephen's Green near the top of Grafton Street to continue my study of *The Course*. We took advantage of the unseasonably warm November afternoon and walked for 30 minutes through the park. We explored much of its 22 acres, crossing over O'Connell Bridge and visiting the Yeats Memorial Gardens with its beautiful sculpture of Ireland's beloved poet and 1923 Nobel Prize winner, William Butler Yeats, crafted by Sir Henry Moore, the English artist and sculpture. We also paused to admire the bust of James Joyce which faces his former University College at Newman House.

During our walk through St. Stephen's Green, Ajay coached me on how to become centered in truth and peace. He told me that being centered in truth requires us to "spend time and energy living our dreams and pursuing our goals." He added, "If you are not spending your time living your truth and pursuing your dreams, you are not in concert with your Inner Spirit."

The second part of the equation is being centered in peace. On this subject, Ajay told me, "*The Course* reminds us that *peace within* is only possible if your Inner Spirit is guiding you through life instead of your ego. *The Course* teaches us that our Inner Spirit is grounded in knowing the way and provides us clarity of direction. This is possible because our Inner Spirit lives in the *now* and responds to our affirmations. This is why it's important that every day you BAG It and remind your Inner Spirit of your goals and desires. Once your Inner Spirit embraces an affirmation, it will set about to make that goal a reality. It does so by enlisting the support of your ego to accomplish that goal. This is the secret power of your Inner Spirit. It can positively influence and guide your ego! Ironically, as your Inner Spirit resurfaces, your ego learns to trust it and support its efforts to help you achieve your vision and goals. The reason the ego will support your vision and goals is this. They represent the *future*—a place where the ego can comfortably reside."

Ajay continued. "But in order to achieve this transformation, it requires more spiritual energy and power than you currently possess. So, you must learn to tap into your Inner Spirit. Only your Inner Spirit has unlimited energy and the power to communicate with the Divine Source. The reason for this is your divineness is centered in your Inner Spirit.

"To achieve this transformation requires extraordinary powers which we all possess but rarely use. But, as *The Course* reminds us, *normal* people never make history! Greatness is reserved for those who do extraordinary things with their talents and abilities. To attain that level, you must have the courage to change and the willingness to act in truth and peace. These are gifts only your Inner Spirit can provide you."

As we sat in one of the white bandstand shelters overlooking a pond, Ajay added, "The key is to become a conscious creator of the universe you desire and the results you seek by connecting with your Inner Spirit. In order to accomplish your desired goals you must respond to this question: *What am I doing each day that will help me achieve my stated mission of finding purpose, peace and passion?* This is the question behind the question.

From this point forward, it is a matter of *intention* and honoring your intentions. We all have good intentions. But, as the axiom suggests, the road to hell is paved with good intentions. Volition is the key to change and to finding your higher purpose, peace and passion in life. Unfortunately, seldom do we convert our intentions into positive actions and meaningful results. I think the reason why is that people lack focus; and this lack of focus and follow-through are the reasons so many well-intentioned people never realize their life dreams."

Ajay stood up and walked a few meters from the bandstand shelter to the edge of the nearby pond where he took a bag of bread crumbs from his coat pocket and sprinkled them on the ground for the birds to eat. He returned to our bandstand and said to me, "Interestingly, achieving your vision, dreams and goals has less to do with your talents and abilities and more to do with focus and discipline. We all have talent and ability but we get distracted and easily discouraged along the way. Someone tells us it can't be done. Or worse, our ego creates doubt in our mind. Most people live average lives. I'm talking about millions of good people who could be great at something, but for a variety of reasons and excuses, they never blossom. They lead their quiet lives of desperation. Why? It's because they are living through their ego and not their Inner Spirit."

Ajay explained it to me this way. *"The Course* teaches us that the mundane tasks of daily life will consume us if we allow only our ego to lead us. In other words, if we devote all our energy to performing the normal, everyday tasks and responsibilities required of us during our Discovery Years and Fulfillment Years, we will be worn out by the time we reach our Legacy Years. Our Success Energy Source—or SES as *The Course* refers to it—will be depleted without the support of our Inner Spirit.

"Also, too often, we allow others, who don't really care about our vision, dreams and ambitions to limit our success by telling us we aren't smart enough or pretty enough; or, we don't have a college degree; or, we weren't a very good parent; or, we're the wrong color or gender; or, we're overweight; or, we're too old. These negative statements and relationships are toxic to achieving our dreams and goals. And yet, for some strange reason, we believe the naysayers and internalize their vitriolic words and sentiments. In essence, we allow other people and their opinions and lies to keep us from achieving our greatness.

"*The Course* teaches us that our Inner Spirit and the Divine Source only think in positive terms. They are our sources of strength and the twin engines we must use to power our ego to help us achieve our dreams. Because we have the gift of free will, it is up to each of us to get out of bed every morning and move towards the fulfillment of our vision, goals and dreams. Of course, we can stay in bed and bemoan the fact that the odds are against us. This reminds me of a funny idiom Dr. Kavi used to emphasize the negativism by which many people live their lives. It goes like this: *Today was to be your lucky day. But due to circumstances under your control, it has been postponed indefinitely.*"

Ajay paused for a moment to look approvingly at the ducks and swans in the pond enjoying his bread crumbs and then told me, "The Divine Source does not roll dice. So, it all comes down to the key questions of *The Course* that we must answer in order to achieve our dreams. First, *How are you living a life worth remembering?* Secondly, *What is your higher purpose in life?* If you cannot answer these questions with complete confidence and certainty, you will drift through life without ever knowing the real reason you exist. Your greatness will go unrealized. Satisfactorily answering the first question is contingent upon answering the second one."

Ajay added, "Those who cannot answer the question, *What is my higher purpose?* will not find peace in their lifetime because peace can only be discovered through the power of Divine Grace and our Inner Spirit. Without peace, you cannot know your higher purpose."

Ajay allowed me to reflect on what he had just told me and then added,

"Finally, if you cannot answer the question, *What is my higher purpose?*, you will never have true passion for the things you do in life. Certainly, you can enjoy a good life without doing these things, but passion is that intrinsic factor in your life that can only be tapped when you awaken every morning with a clear understanding of who you are and why you exist. Knowing this will keep you focused and fill you with such a sense of determination and conviction that nothing can stop you from achieving your goals and living your vision and dreams."

The afternoon sun was beginning to slip below the tree tops surrounding St. Stephen's Green. We zipped up our jackets and Ajay opened his leather journal. He told me, "On the final morning of *The Course* retreat, Dr. Kavi offered these words to help each of us find clarity of direction in our lives. So let me share with you what he told us since it will be helpful to you as you go forward from here:

> *It has been a long day. But I want you to stay with me for just a few more minutes. Be here now. I want you to close your eyes and I want you to look back on your life. I want you to examine those times when you failed to accomplish a goal or realize a particular dream. I want you to see very clearly all those times you were disappointed in life. I know this will be very difficult for some of you because it is painful to revisit failure and disappointment. But give yourself permission to do this one last time.*
>
> *As you examine your life's failures and disappointments, I want you to look closely at these moments in your life and ask yourself one very important question. Is there one person who is always there? Who do you see there at the scene of the crime? I'm talking about the crime of disappointment; the crime of lost opportunity; the crime of forgotten dreams and unfulfilled aspirations. Who do you see there? Scan the crowd carefully. Take a hard look. Do you see someone's face you recognize? Someone you know is there. Find them. Now, look into their*

eyes. Who is that person standing there? Do you recognize him or her? Look closely now.

Ah yes, it is you. There is no one else who was always there in these moments of failure and disappointment, was there? It was always you. For no one else can bear the blame for your failures and disappointments, but you—only you.

But wait a minute. I want you to look closely at that person for just another moment. Something is different. What is it? It is becoming clearer in your mind's picture, isn't it? How interesting. The person you see at the scene is not the same 'you' sitting here in this room, is it? No. It is the old you. It is an image of you from the past. It is a 'you' who was not loved as you are loved today. It is a 'you' who was unwilling to take risks because you did not have the courage to act on your dreams as you have done so today. It is a 'you' who would not allow yourself to be successful because you only relied on your ego and did not know how to reach your Inner Spirit and open your heart to discover and achieve your higher purpose. But now you do.

Your eyes are still closed. Take a deep breath and relax now. Roll your shoulders a few times and relax your neck. Breathe. Ask your Inner Spirit to be present and forgive that 'old you' as it turns and walks away—out of your life forever.

Continue to breathe deeply and inhale fully. Are you ready to meet the 'new you?' If tears need to be shed to wash away the negative images and painful, destructive memories of the old you, now is the time to release them. Do it now as the 'old you' walks further away—and leaves you forever. It is taking with it all those negative images, those painful moments and destructive memories. It is leaving now. There it goes. It's moving farther away, out of your conscious and subconscious mind.

10,000 Days

Now, it is gone forever.

Breathe deeply and inhale fully. Now exhale smoothly and relax. Take your hand and gently touch your face. If there are tears on your cheeks, wipe them away. You are now safe and among new friends who support you, accept you and love you for who you really are.

Your eyes are still closed, but not too tightly. Gently, relaxed. Now, there is a new image I want you to visualize in your mind. It is the new you. I want you to picture in your mind the 'new you.' You look fabulous! You have dreams and goals. You have the power to achieve success. You possess the gifts and talents to achieve everything in life you want to achieve. You only need to do two things to make your vision a reality; and they are to believe it is possible and then act on it. Rely on your Inner Spirit for courage and grace. As you greet your 'new' you, I want you to embrace him or her. I want you to say to the 'new' you, you have my permission to dream. You have my permission to succeed in life. You will succeed and achieve your dreams because you have the exact talents and gifts necessary to succeed. Open your heart to new possibilities.

Now, I want you to open your eyes, stand up and repeat after me:
I now release all my doubts, hesitations, fears, and excuses for failure to the past. I let them go forever.
In their place I recite my new affirmations:
I am the 'new' me. It is the only me that exists.
I believe in me.
I am willing and able to change in order to succeed.
I have the power to succeed. I believe in me without reservation.
I am capable of achieving my dreams and life goals.
I am focused on my goals.
I have a higher purpose.
I listen to my Inner Spirit because it is always truthful.
Together, we are moving forward to achieve my goals and my dreams.

I can feel success.

I believe in me completely!

I know my higher purpose is rooted in love—love of self and everything good I experience.

I am at peace with myself.

I am passionate about my new life!

It is my right and my destiny to achieve my dreams and goals!

I believe in me completely!

My new life begins now!

I reflected on the powerful words Ajay read to me from his journal. I felt renewed and liberated by Dr. Kavi's words. A sense of peace came over me as if my Inner Spirit had surfaced and was ready to guide me to The Kingdom of Roses. I felt confident that I could confront the Four Stones. It was a fitting end to our time together in Dublin and I knew I was ready to take on the next challenge of *The Course.*

As we left St. Stephen's Green, Ajay gave me the final assignment for *The Course.* It consisted of two questions to prepare me for entering The Kingdom of Roses. First, *What do you choose to create in your life during the next 100 days?* If you can define the goals you want to achieve in the next 100 days—like your net worth, your state of health, places to travel, the state of your relations with people you care about and the state of your own well-being—then you can achieve great results.

Secondly, *Do you treat yourself the way you want others to treat you?* One of the things I learned about myself is that others are not going to treat me any better than I treat myself. This includes not only physical characteristics such as health, weight and appearance, but also mental and psychological states. Remember that *The Course* teaches us that we are the sum of our parts. So every aspect of our being needs to be in alignment in order for us to fully realize our higher purpose and attain our divineness.

As we walked back to the Four Seasons Hotel, Ajay asked me if I was still planning to research my family's Irish roots during my visit to Ireland. I told him I was off to Wexford in the morning, then onto Westport in County Mayo on Friday for that very purpose. Ajay suggested that while in Wexford, I meet with Liam and Anna Kennedy. Also, he encouraged me to visit Michael and Maeve Brennan in Westport. Ajay told me Liam and Michael used to work for TGC and both could offer me valuable insight on my final assignments since they had previously completed *The Course.* Ajay told me he would arrange for my visits and I agreed to meet them.

CHAPTER 28

The Wexford Conversation

I departed the Four Seasons Dublin the next morning and headed south to Wexford. Armed with tidbits of information about my family's Irish roots, I made the leisurely drive to Wexford where my father's ancestors settled after emigrating from England in the 1100s. I arrived at the Whitford House Hotel in Wexford in time for lunch and ventured into the Forthside Bar & Bistro where I met Anna and Liam Kennedy.

They were born in Wexford and had traveled to every continent except Antarctica. They graduated from Trinity College in Dublin where Liam also earned his Masters Degree.

Shortly after graduating from college, Liam and Anna were married and left Ireland to work in the United States. Liam accepted a job with TGC in California while Anna taught high school and eventually joined the faculty of the University of Southern California after completing her doctorate. According to Liam, he spent 36 wonderful years with TGC including 12 as their CEO. When he retired, Liam and Anna returned to Wexford.

Only after Liam revealed his background did I fully understand the close connection between him and Ajay. I also learned that Liam and Anna had completed *The Course* with Dr. Kavi in Mumbai five years earlier. As we ate lunch, Anna told me how *The Course* had enriched their lives during that time.

"When we completed *The Course*, Liam and I were in our Legacy Years so our belief systems were firmly established. Change did not come easy. But *The Course* challenged us to re-examine our beliefs. Dr. Kavi told us 'our B.S.'—as he refers to a person's Belief Systems—is what holds us back. Our beliefs cause us to be spiritually constipated!"

"The problem so many Baby Boomers have," Liam interjected, "is how do we challenge what we have believed for so long? Yes, we want to find meaning in our lives. But this requires us to be open to new ideas and possibilities. Changing *how* one thinks and opening your heart to new answers is very difficult because we are resistant to change. The more Anna and I probed to find the root cause of our inaction and self-imposed limitations, the more we realized it was due to our beliefs. *The Course* helped Anna and me understand why certain beliefs were emotionally and spiritually destructive to achieving our goals and dreams. Also, we began to understand why people live *in lack* instead of abundance."

"So I take it you don't accept the argument that God will solve our problems?" I asked. Liam pounced on my question and responded with laughter. "God doesn't solve problems. God doesn't have any problems! Only people have problems! You see, Tom, one of the reasons God created men and women is He loves stories! Despite the fact that we are born perfect, we slowly self-destruct with each passing day because we allow our ego to suffocate our Inner Spirit. On the other hand, the Divine Source is perfect.

But to solve your problems, you don't need God's help. You just need to go deep within yourself and find meaningful, truth-based answers. Your Inner Spirit, which is linked to the Divine Source, will guide you. *The Course* refers to this process as remapping your life. It's about reasoning, thinking and elevating one's self to a higher state of consciousness. Our Inner Spirit will reveal the truth to us. The truth is there, but it's hidden deep within our subconscious. Your Inner Spirit will reveal the truth if you ask. This is why *The Course* teaches us to think and reason for ourselves. It's the only way to discover the truth."

Liam sipped his wine and then asked me, "Tom, are you familiar with Reiki, the Japanese technique for stress reduction and relaxation that promotes healing?"

I had heard of Reiki but never practiced it. I told Liam so.

"You might consider it," Anna noted. "It's a spiritual practice developed in 1922 by Dr. Mikao Usui. It's administered by laying on hands and is based on the idea that an unseen life force energy—which *The Course* refers to as the Divine Source—flows through us and is what causes us to be alive. If one's life force energy is low, then we are more likely to get sick or feel stress. If it is high, we are more capable of being happy and healthy."

Liam added, "The word Reiki is made of two Japanese words: *Rei* which means God's Wisdom or the Higher Power and *Ki* which is life force energy. Thus, Reiki can be translated as *spiritually guided life force energy*."

"During *The Course* retreat," Anna said, "we were introduced to the Usui system of Reiki because it includes an active commitment to improve oneself. This is in harmony with what *The Course* teaches us. Let me share with you a poem by Dr. Mikao Usui that reinforces the significance of living a life of balance."

> *The secret art of inviting happiness*
> *The miraculous medicine of all diseases*
> *Just for today, do not anger*
> *Do not worry and be filled with gratitude*
> *Devote yourself to your work. Be kind to people.*
> *Every morning and evening, join your hands in prayer.*
> *Pray these words to your heart*
> *and chant these words with your mouth.*

Anna added, "I share this with you because most people do not fully appreciate *who* they are. We go through life with little more than an elementary understanding of ourselves. *The Course* teaches us that we are spiritual beings who are part of a universal field of energy and consciousness. I think Heraclites, the Greek philosopher, said it best about those people who do not think for themselves or use their higher powers. 'What sense or thought do they have? They follow the popular singers, and they take the crowd as their teacher.'

"*The Course* teaches us that who we really are extends far beyond our aging bodies. The *real you* lives within your Inner Spirit. This is why connecting with your Inner Spirit is the ultimate key to achieving purpose, peace and passion in life. There is a difference between believing in something and accepting the unexplainable on the basis of faith. What distinguishes mankind from the animal kingdom is our ability to think, reason and love. This is why our universal belief system has evolved over the millennia and is based on our ability to reason, think and prove our conclusions. It is not based on an emotional quotient. As we change and evolve we become enlightened. This is how we progress beyond the primordial, instinctive emotions of fear and survival.

"Again, I think Heraclites understood this concept when he said, 'No one can step twice into the same river, nor touch mortal substance twice in the same condition. By the speed of its change, it scatters and gathers again.' By design, we should constantly be changing and evolving as spiritual beings."

Liam commented, "*The Course* reaffirmed for me that I was ego-driven. It also clarified that I lacked a channel through which I could convey my love and support for people because I had an under-developed relationship with my Inner Spirit. *The Course* helped me fully appreciate this fact and revealed the path to me. So this is why I encourage people to be tenacious and use their mind powers to live their dreams and create peace in their life. When you call upon your Inner Spirit, it hears your petitions and surfaces to show you the way. Initially, we all seek help in answering the same two questions because everyone wants to live a life worth remembering. Those questions are: *Why do I exist?* and *How do I live my higher purpose?"*

Anna edged forward and said softly, "When you can answer those questions, you are ready to enter The Kingdom of Roses. I am talking about that metaphysical place where the Divine Source dwells and we exist in a spiritual state of Divine Grace that is attainable by anyone who can successfully cross over the Bridge of Forgiveness and overturn the Four Stones. It is that place where we can access our spiritual powers, attain peace and discover an unparalleled degree of contentment and happiness in our life. Once there, mastering the seven petals of the rose, which Ajay shared with you, is the key to living your higher purpose each and every day."

Anna sipped her wine then added, "Of course, once you enter The Kingdom of Roses your work is not finished. You must still live your higher purpose. That is why *The Course* emphasizes the importance of mastering the seven petals of the rose. By mastering each of the seven petals, you strengthen your commitment to living your higher purpose and ultimately, this is how you achieve your special relationship with the Divine Source and move closer to the highest level of self-actualizing and realizing your wholeness."

Liam smiled admiringly at his wife and said, "Let me tell you how to overcome the Four Stones of Anger, Greed, Lust and Envy. You must live your beliefs and those beliefs must be tried and tested. You cannot be indifferent in terms of what you believe. Your values must be strong enough to sustain you in your moments of doubt and struggle. From time to time, you will succumb to one or more of the Four Stones.

It's part of our human frailty. It's the ego's way of trying to keep us in that velvet rut called contentment. But you must be strong and resist its lure. This is why *The Course* devotes so many exercises and lessons to the Four Stones. Remember that overcoming Anger, Greed, Lust and Envy is part of our human growth process. Without such challenges there would be no reason for us to change and improve ourselves. It is through our struggle to continuously improve that we discover and reach that state of union with the Divine Source. It's important to remember the Divine Source is both imminent and transcendent."

Anna commented, "Remember, you already have everything you need to achieve greatness. But you must practice sharing your gifts with others. Be a giver and then allow others to give their best to you. There is a wonderful poem we learned at *The Course* retreat. I don't recall the author, but it goes like this:

> *Every problem is a question trying to resolve itself.*
>
> *Every question is an answer trying to discover itself.*
>
> *Every answer is an action trying to transform itself into a way of life.*

As the waitress served dessert Anna continued. "*The Course* reminds us that what we truly value does not come from what we own, but rather from our spiritual essence. When you tap into that essence and begin to live your higher purpose, you will know you have entered The Kingdom of Roses. Remember that life is an investment in yourself and by nurturing your mind and soul you are caring for yourself. No one else is going to do that for you because no one else can. No one will ever care as much about you as you do.

But once you invest in yourself by nurturing your Inner Spirit, others will naturally respond to your positive energy and liveliness. This explains the mystery of how someone is attracted to another person and how they can openly support our dreams and higher purpose. This is how the cycle of fulfillment and life satisfaction work. The beautiful thing about this life fulfillment cycle is that once you have taken care of yourself and you begin to care for others, abundance will flow in your direction because your capacity to love and give of yourself is returned many times over. This is the ultimate gift we yearn for—to love ourselves and accept others—because it makes us complete. Of course, this special gift is hidden inside each of us.

For many people, it lies there dormant like a beautiful diamond that is never discovered because it remains buried under the rock we are sitting on. It is suppressed by our ego and only our Inner Spirit can reveal it. This is why it is so important to have balance between our ego and Inner Spirit and allow our Inner Spirit to surface and guide us. It is through our Inner Spirit that we achieve our dreams and live a life worth remembering."

Liam nodded in agreement and said, "Saint Matthew tells us, 'Neither do people light a lamp and put it under a bowl. Instead, they put it on its stand and it gives light to everyone in the house. In the same way, let your light shine before men, that they may see your good deeds.'"

As Liam nibbled on a piece of caramel chocolate dessert, he added, "*The Course* challenges us in this regard by asking: What is it *right now* that you choose to do in order to move closer to achieving your dreams and live your higher purpose?"

Liam let me think about what he had said for a moment and then added with a smile, "This is a very important question. Consider this fact. All of life has prepared you for this very moment. This is why you are here with us in Wexford this very day!"

It was at that moment I realized all my somedays were today.

Anna read my mind and said to me, "We are a gift to each other. I'm reminded of the Nigerian musician Babatunde Olatunji's delightful poem. It goes:

Yesterday is history.

Tomorrow is a mystery. And today? Today is a gift.

That is why we call it the present.

Before we concluded our lunch, Anna gave me a present. I peeled away the wrapping paper to find a beautiful soft brown leather-covered book entitled, *The Kingdom of Roses: The Secret to Living Your Higher Purpose*. It looked like a collector's edition. I thumbed through the short book and glimpsed several pages of beautiful artwork and quotations. It was co-authored by Kavi Chavan, M.D. and Anna Kennedy, Ph.D. I thanked her and promised to read it before leaving Ireland.

As we left the restaurant and walked through the gardens of the Whitford House Hotel, Liam confirmed my meeting with Michael and Maeve Brennan the next evening in Westport, County Mayo. Liam told me that Michael had worked for TGC's Irish operations in Dublin for 22 years before retiring. He and his wife, Maeve, were graduates of *The Course*. They completed it three years ago and now facilitated *The Course* retreats in Dublin.

Anna said, "Michael can shed some light on the two questions we discussed at lunch today: *Why do I exist?* and *How do I live my higher purpose?*"

I told Liam and Anna I looked forward to meeting the Brennans. Liam took the liberty of making a hotel reservation for me at the Knockranny House in Westport. Anna suggested I meet the Brennans for dinner at La Fougère in the Knockranny House. She said it was "the best restaurant in all of County Mayo!"

I thanked my hosts and bid them goodbye. I spent the remainder of my afternoon researching my father's Irish roots. That evening I perused *The Kingdom of Roses: The Secret to Living Your Higher Purpose*. As I fell asleep, my head was full of beautiful images and quotes about this spiritual place I yearned to visit.

CHAPTER 29

The Westport Conversation

The next morning I drove 160 miles through some of the most beautiful countryside I had ever seen. I stopped in Galway briefly to shop at Ó'Máille's for authentic Irish sweaters. Then, I continued on to Westport. Anna had encouraged me to enjoy the Knockranny House's Spa Salveo, so I did. At 6:30 pm, I made my way downstairs to La Fougère where I met Michael and Maeve Brennan.

Michael recounted his history with TGC. He had graduated from the National University of Ireland (NIU) in Galway with a degree in Economics. He also earned his Masters Degree there. In 1980, he was hired by TGC when they established their first plant in Dublin. He eventually rose to the position of Director of Irish Operations in 1991 and oversaw TGC's three facilities in Dublin, Cork and Belfast until his retirement. Despite the fact that he was only 46, Michael decided to retire after 22 years with TGC so he could fulfill his dream and teach economics at NUI in Galway. He told me he wanted to teach while he was still able to ride a bicycle across campus!

Michael shared with me that he had two life-altering experiences in 2003. The first was his introduction to *The Course* and meeting Dr. Kavi Chavan in Mumbai that spring. The second was meeting the woman he would later marry at *The Course* retreat in Dublin. Dr. Anna Kennedy had introduced Michael to Maeve.

It was obvious from their interaction that Michael had found his spiritual partner and compass in Maeve. She was vivacious, talkative and animated. Maeve complimented her soft-spoken husband perfectly. Her long red hair and freckles gave Maeve a youthful appearance. Michael teased that Maeve was half his age although she later confessed that she had recently celebrated her 40th birthday.

Maeve was born and raised in Ballina, which is the largest city in County Mayo and home of the famous River Moy and St. Muredach's Cathedral. She completed her undergraduate degree at Trinity College in Dublin and earned her graduate degree at Cambridge's Clare Hall College. She also earned her Doctor of Letters from Cambridge. She loved teaching Literature to her Cambridge students, but made the difficult decision to resign her faculty position and return to County Mayo to be closer to her ailing mother and two younger sisters. Maeve was fortunate to land a job as a World Literature professor at NUI Galway where she now teaches. As a mother, she confided that her professorial duties take a back seat to raising their son.

As we enjoyed an elegant dinner at La Fougère, Maeve and Michael talked openly about *The Course* and shared their thoughts on the two questions that brought me to Westport in search of answers.

"I think it's simply a matter of receptivity on the part of each person who tries to find their higher purpose in life," Maeve told me. "What really captured my attention during *The Course* retreat was our discussion on how it is possible to attain a state of lasting peace and happiness in life. Dr. Leif Livingheart refers to it as Reasonless Joy. I very much wanted that for myself. At the time I was troubled by those two nagging questions:

10,000 Days

Why do I exist? and How do I live my higher purpose?"

Michael noted, "*The Course* teaches us that we exist to live our higher purpose. So, the challenge is to discover your higher purpose. In this way, your life can have both meaning and purpose. I agree with Edgar Cayce's statement, 'Soul development should take precedence over all things.'"

Maeve replied, "Leo Buscaglia wrote, 'It's not enough to have lived. We should be determined to live for something.' When you allow your Inner Spirit to resonate with your ego, you will finally meet the real you and experience your whole self. Until that occurs, I believe your life is disingenuous because it is incomplete. The frustrating thing is that we sense something is missing but we don't know what it is or how to identify it."

"Well," Michael added, "for most people I think it is a matter of making decisions that are heart-centered instead of decisions that are ego-driven and reactionary. Dr. Kavi defines it this way:

> *The quality of every person's life depends on their decision-making abilities because every decision leads to an action. Every action leads to an outcome which is either positive or negative. If you elevate your decision-making process, you will increase the probability of making better decisions and, therefore, your success in life.*

"Making good decisions is the key to creating higher levels of satisfaction in your life. But how do we make good decisions instead of mediocre or bad decisions? According to *The Course*, we must be balanced. In other words, there is equal input from both the ego and the Inner Spirit. It cannot be a lopsided, emotionally-charged decision-making process."

Michael continued, "During *The Course* retreat we discussed Aristotle's four levels of happiness and how superficial happiness can be for some people. The first level is *Happiness as a Thing*. Aristotle referred to this level as *Laetus*. This kind of happiness is based on immediate gratification and very common among children. For example, 'I see candy. I like candy. I eat the candy.' It's gone and I'm on to the next thing that pleases me."

"I find the second level of happiness very interesting," Maeve volunteered, "because it's all about comparison. Aristotle referred to it as *Felix* but Dr. Kavi calls it *Comparative Happiness*. It's about keeping up with the Jones! At level two, our happiness is dependent upon how much *we* have compared to our friends and neighbors. Western culture champions *Comparative Happiness* because western society is based on capitalism, which relies on consumption. The problem is that these two levels are completely ego-driven and self-serving. This is why they cannot sustain long-term happiness."

"The third level of happiness," Michael offered, "is the happiness we derive from seeing the good that happens to others. Aristotle calls it *Beatitudo*. Dr. Kavi refers to this level as the *Happiness of Blessings* and links his *Givers Gain* principle to it. This level of happiness begins to move us from an ego-based state of happiness to one that is rooted in our Inner Spirit."

"The one thing we must be careful of with the third level of happiness," Maeve interjected, "is not to become dependent upon others for our own happiness and satisfaction. When you rely on others for your happiness, eventually you'll be disappointed because it's only satisfying as long as other people are prospering. When they falter, suffer or die, your state of happiness is negatively affected and declines. This is often the case when a parent or spouse dies unexpectedly. We slip into a state of depression or melancholy and withdraw."

Maeve continued. "Aristotle's fourth level of happiness is *Sublime Beatitudo*. Dr. Kavi refers to this level as the *Happiness of Fulfillment*. It embraces the concept of self-fulfillment and perfection in life. It is closely linked to the attributes of purpose, peace and passion that you will experience in The Kingdom of Roses. People who attain *Sublime Beatitudo* exist in a transcendental state of beauty, truth and love. Ironically, these are the three qualities that most people find very difficult to celebrate on a consistent basis because they can only be sustained by our Inner Spirit."

"*The Course* reminds us," Michael pointed out, "that no one intentionally chooses to be miserable. We all seek happiness in life. But when Maeve and I measured our state of happiness against Aristotle's four levels of happiness, it was apparent that something was missing. Only we had failed to discover what that *something* was."

Maeve politely interrupted by squeezing Michael's hand. "*The Course* taught us that you need to ask the question: *What is it that leads people to discovery?* I think it's some kind of '*SEE* Experience'—that is, a Significant Emotional Experience. When people undergo a significant emotional experience it opens their eyes and their heart. It creates insight. Insight, in turn, creates new pathways for learning and helps people transform themselves. But until people pull themselves out of their Velvet Rut—that detrimental state of contentment and comfort—they will not grow or evolve. Instead, they'll atrophy and regress. It's just human nature."

Michael added, "In business terms, we often talk about the FUD factor as the leading reason for management indecision and corporate inertia. FUD stands for Fear, Uncertainty and Doubt. I think this also applies to our personal lives. When TGC introduced me to the neuropsychology of leadership as advocated by Warren Benis and Burt Nanus, I realized that several of their ten characteristics of great leaders were also applicable to one's personal life. I'm talking about characteristics such as mastery of self, the management of change, creating a climate for your vision and making your vision a reality. These are characteristics that also relate to our personal quest for happiness and fulfillment."

"Initiating change," Maeve suggested, "begins with awareness and an awakening experience as Michael mentioned. It was Henri Bergson who said, 'To exist is to change; to change is to mature; and to mature is to go on creating oneself endlessly.'

"So, when you ask yourself those two questions—*Why do I exist?* and *How do I live my higher purpose?*—it is more often out of a sense of discomfort or unhappiness. The more unhappy or uncomfortable you are, the sooner you start seeking answers to these two questions. This, in turn, causes us to change as Henri Bergson suggests."

Michael took out his diary and removed a sheet of paper. He drew a bell-shaped curve. Then he said, "During *The Course* retreat, Dr. Kavi drew a bell-shaped curve on the board. One end of the curve was labeled *Survival* and represented about 15% of the population. Dr. Kavi then labeled the middle 70% of the curve as the *Amorphous Middle*. The extreme end of the curve was labeled *Success* and comprised about 15% of the population. Looking at this bell-shaped curve, one would assume that only those people in the *Survival* percentage struggled with life. In fact, everyone struggles with some phase of their life. According to Dr. Kavi, no matter where you are on this bell-shaped curve of life, you face challenges and struggles.

Some of us struggle to survive financially while others struggle with issues like love, happiness or career success. Ultimately, as we move along the curve, our life goals change. We progress through our Discovery Years, our Fulfillment Years and our Legacy Years. In each phase of life, the struggles we encounter are different. But there is always a struggle. We struggle from survival to satisfaction; from success to significance; and ultimately, from wisdom to sustained enlightenment."

"I remember that bell-shaped curve," Maeve commented. "When I first saw it, I was reminded of Henry Ward Beecher's comment on life's struggles. He said, 'Suffering is part of the divine idea.' In other words, the Divine Source made us so we would struggle, suffer, conquer and thrive. In this way, we fully appreciate the magnificence of life and the joy of discovering and living our higher purpose."

Maeve sipped her wine then added, "Another thing about that bell-shaped curve example is the indisputable fact that everyone faces struggles and challenges as they progress through the various phases of life. Specifically, I'm talking about struggles with relationships, the challenge of growing older, continuously learning, confronting contentment, being coachable, achieving gratification, enlightenment and ultimately, attaining fulfillment in life. It was your American president Teddy Roosevelt who reminded us, 'It is only through labor and painful effort, by grim energy and resolute courage that we move on to better things.'"

Michael reflected on Maeve's words and added, "*The Course* teaches us that there is but one universal answer to the question. *Why do I exist?* The answer is to achieve a state of wholeness or consciousness in this lifetime. However, as long as your ego is in the driver's seat, it is impossible to achieve wholeness. I like how Dr. Kavi described this challenge to a group of software executives. He said that life would be so much easier if we just had the source code!"

"What I'm hearing you tell me is that somewhere along the journey, we must decide—in the words of Teilhard de Chardin—whether 'we are human beings having a spiritual experience, or spiritual beings having a human experience,'" I suggested.

"Yes, I think that's an important part of the equation," Maeve replied. "But actually, we are both because we have an ego and an Inner Spirit. However, when you quote the great French mystic and priest, Teilhard de Chardin, I think it's important to also remember what he said about living our higher purpose. He told us, 'Someday, after mastering the winds, the waves, the tides and gravity, we shall harness for God the energies of love; and then, for a second time in the history of the world, man will have discovered fire!'"

As the waiter cleared our dinner plates and served us tea, Michael offered a final thought on the subject. "Heraclites said, 'Much learning does not teach understanding.' *The Course* reminds us that knowing our destination is half the journey. This is why discovering our higher purpose is essential to living a life worth remembering. And to reach that level of enlightenment we must allow our Inner Spirit to guide us because enlightenment emanates from our Inner Spirit.

While it periodically surfaces throughout our life, our challenge is to recognize it in those special moments and listen carefully to what our Inner Spirit is trying to tell us. This is how we progress along the spectrum of that bell-shaped curve Dr. Kavi described during *The Course* retreat. Otherwise, I think we're flying blind and making decisions intuitively instead of with the counsel and wisdom of our Inner Spirit."

"Well, therein lays the conundrum called Life," countered Maeve. "We are human and spiritual beings comprised of an ego and an Inner Spirit. So, both components of our Being must participate in our life. Unfortunately, our ego thinks its job is to keep us guessing while our Inner Spirit knows the truth and tries to reveal it to us in subtle ways. However, when you're struggling with everything life throws at you—your job, finances, friends, family, relationships and your own Four Stones— it's not easy. Our ego clouds the picture and causes us to postpone decisions.

For those who are struggling and trying to get past the survival phase, the question of how we choose to live our higher purpose never enters into the equation. Those people just aren't there yet. But that doesn't mean we should give up because living a life of regrets is far worse than struggling through the transformation of self-discovery. *The Course* teaches us that the greatest pain we can ever suffer is self-inflicted. It is the pain of regret."

I nodded my agreement as our conversation ended. Nothing more needed to be said. We watched the fire burn brightly in the dining room fireplace and drank our tea. I thanked Michael and Maeve for the wonderful evening and for sharing their insights on the two questions of *The Course*. They had given me much to ponder. I returned to my guest room where I made notes for more than an hour while the conversation

10,000 Days

was still fresh in my mind. I also read more of Anna Kennedy and Dr. Kavi's book, *The Kingdom of Roses: The Secret to Living Your Higher Purpose* before drifting off to sleep.

On Saturday morning, I relaxed at the Knockranny House's Spa Salveo and checked out at 12 noon. After researching my mother's Irish roots that afternoon, I drove to Dublin that evening and checked into the Clontarf Castle Hotel near the airport where I reviewed my notes from my dinners with the Kennedys and Brennans and packed my suitcase for my return flight to California. I had bought a number of gifts and souvenirs, so I was concerned about my luggage weighing too much. Then, it occurred to me I was flying in a private jet! So I visited the hotel gift shop and purchased an extra carry-on bag to hold all my extra stuff. No problem!

On Sunday afternoon, I met the TGC entourage at Dublin Airport's executive jet terminal where we departed for our flight to California. Ajay and I huddled in BBJ-3's conference room for two hours as I talked about my dinner discussions with the Kennedys and Brennans. Ajay listened intently as I replayed our conversations and what I had learned from them. As I concluded, Ajay nodded his approval and told me he had three new assignments to help me master *The Course* and access The Kingdom of Roses over the next 100 days. He waited until we were across the Atlantic Ocean before revealing the new assignments.

Part Four

Embracing the
Power of Love

CHAPTER 30

The 100-Day Plan

S omewhere over the east coast, Ajay gave me three final assignments for *The Course.* The first assignment was to create my 100-Day Plan to help me practice the principles and concepts of *The Course.* This was a project every student of *The Course* completes to ensure we remain committed to our life goals. He gave me a worksheet that identified the eight elements of the 100-Day Plan: Spirituality, Relationships, Environment, Money, Romance, Fun & Recreation, Career and Wellness.

Ajay told me this plan would be a preface to my *Life Plan for Success*®, another powerful tool from *The Course.* The *Life Plan for Success*® encompasses the eight dimensions of the 100-Day Plan and also includes other critical elements such as my Mission Statement, a Defining Statement for my work, several one-sentence Intentions or Annual Resolutions and a strategy to achieve my monetary goals and a closing Statement of Success & Achievement that I would sign and update every 30 days.

The Course teaches us that while it is possible to become what you think about, you must first commit to your goals through your intentions—

then convert those intentions into action. Without this important second step, your life is reduced to wishing and hoping for results. Of course, *hope* is not a strategy! It's important to be confident and hopeful, but success in life requires a greater commitment. It requires us to use certain tools like the *Life Plan for Success*® to create our desired outcomes.

My second assignment was an exercise Ajay called the *Walking Meditation*. Every day for 30 minutes, Ajay asked me to walk in a quiet setting and recite one of five mantras he gave me. Through the *Walking Meditation* exercise, I increased my ability to communicate with my Inner Spirit and, in turn, achieve a deeper connection with the Divine Source. Within a few weeks, I began to see the world in a more positive light. I also developed a keen sense of appreciation and respect for people and nature.

Ajay recommended two mantras for me to recite when certain situations dictated a calmer response. The first mantra was "Ramma, Ramma, Ramma" which he instructed me to repeat 10 times whenever I got angry. The second mantra was "Hreem, Hreem, Hreem" which I was to repeat whenever I felt myself growing impatient or frustrated. Ajay explained that these mantras were created a thousand years ago as a way to channel energy from the physical self to the Inner Spirit and connect one with the Divine Source. These mantras could alter my state of mind and redirect my emotional responses from anger, frustration or resentment to one of calm and tranquility.

The *Walking Meditation* was also a nice complement to my BAG It exercise which I performed every morning. Over time, I better understood the power of my mantras and how they helped me connect with the energy of universal love and accept people for who they are at this moment.

Eventually, I progressed to the BAGEL exercise which includes the elements of the BAG It exercise and adds the "E" for Expectations and the "L" for Liabilities. Equally important, I found that the *Walking Meditation* helped dissolve my anger, invigorate my spirit, heal my heart and provide the strength I needed on my journey to achieve my life goals. Ajay explained that reciting a mantra was a proven method to help people unleash the power of intention. In other words, what we think and say affects our physiology and moves us closer to achieving our vision, goals and dreams. Thus, it complemented my *Life Plan for Success*®. The *Walking Meditation* also prepared me for Ajay's third assignment, which *The Course* refers to as *Conscious Delight.*

Ajay reminded me that as I progressed through *The Course,* I would experience the three stages of Being. These stages are derived from the ancient Hindu scriptures known as the Upanishads that comprise the core teachings of Vedanta. The three stages of Being that *The Course* teaches are: Existence, Consciousness and Delight. As I focused on the Three Sacred Questions, I was experiencing Existence. As I crossed the Bridge of Forgiveness and mastered the Seven Petals of the Rose, I was experiencing Consciousness. Now, as I prepared to enter The Kingdom of Roses and connect with my intrinsically divine nature, I would experience Delight.

To achieve *Conscious Delight*, I had to master a three-step process that combined the physical, verbal and mental states of meditation. First, I performed the BAGEL exercise—my Blessings, Accomplishments, Goals, Expectations and Liabilities—to ensure I was focused on the here-and-now. Second, I performed the *Walking Meditation* as a way to quiet my mind with a series of mantras and position myself as a witness to life and nature rather than an intruder.

Finally, I used *The Sounds of Silence* exercise which I had learned months before to sit peacefully still for 10 minutes each day and commune with my Inner Spirit. Ajay told me, "The Divine Source and nature have no time limitations. Only humans impose the element of time on themselves. Through the exercise of *Conscious Delight* you can escape time and exist exclusively in the presence of nature and the Divine Source."

My goal was to merge my external consciousness with my Inner Spirit in an effort to achieve a higher level of consciousness or Reasonless Joy. Ajay told me that there are seven states of Consciousness ranging from the lowest level known as Deep, Dreamless Sleep to the highest level known as Cosmic Consciousness. According to Dr. Kavi, it is believed that less than a few hundred people have ever achieved the seventh state of consciousness, also referred to as Integration. Some of the best known names among this select group probably include Jesus, Buddha, Krishna, Thomas Aquinas, Gandhi and Thomas Jefferson.

I had been practicing my meditation exercises for several months, when one morning I felt myself briefly enter that state of *Conscious Delight*. My Inner Spirit controlled my thoughts and I experienced the transformation of my human dimension and connected with my divineness. This state of *Conscious Delight* is something that must be experienced in order to be fully appreciated. I ultimately achieved that level of union with my divineness. I can only explain it to you as a soothing, peaceful feeling that permeated my entire consciousness and elevated me to a different space mentally and emotionally.

While I physically remained still, I could sense a profound metaphysical transformation occurring within me. I could see the image of the Divine Source—an energy so radiant I had to squeeze my eyes tightly so as not to be blinded by the array of brilliant colors flashing before me. After a few seconds, the image was gone and I gradually returned to a state of awakened consciousness that I would define as the *present* or *normal*.

Ajay told me that once I had achieved *Conscious Delight* my life would be forever changed because I could return to this level of consciousness many times and experience great things. For example, Ajay told me people who can repeatedly experience *Conscious Delight* have the power to release their worries and anxieties. Also, they know no fear. He also told me that the more I could exist in a state of *Conscious Delight* the more I would experience a degree of alignment in my life where things would happen in a synchronistic pattern.

"When you are connected with your Inner Spirit," Ajay instructed, "the Divine Source enters your life in mysterious and wonderful ways. You don't need to be in a state of *Conscious Delight*, but when you are, your prayers and desires are answered more quickly."

Some people might argue that the occurrence of such events is simply a matter of coincidence. But *The Course* teaches us there is a divine correlation between everything we experience and living our higher purpose. In other words, our life is not a series of random acts that happen one after another. Instead, what happens in our life is the direct result of our state of consciousness. Some people remain *unconscious* and ignore their Inner Spirit. For these people, life just happens through random, unsynchronized events. They never experience their divineness on earth let alone achieve their higher purpose.

For those of us who are striving to understand ourselves and achieve purpose, peace and passion in our lives, our Inner Spirit will surface and trigger a series of well-timed, orchestrated events that can help us create positive outcomes. And while any one of these events might seem trivial or insignificant at the time, when you piece them all together, you quickly realize that A plus B plus C plus D does, in fact, lead to the results you desire!

The Course reminds us that life is complicated mostly by our own doing. The ego enjoys creating conundrums because complexity confuses our mind and prevents us from taking decisive action. *The Course* teaches us that in order to initiate change and transform ourselves into the person we want to become, we must summon our Inner Spirit to help us solve life's problems and simplify our life. Left to its own devices, the ego will not solve our problems. *The Course* reminds us that the solution to every problem we face is within us.

To bring about major change in our life requires great strength, courage and determination. Only our Inner Spirit is capable of connecting with the Divine Source to help us succeed in times of trouble and profound need. Only our Inner Spirit can bestow upon us the grace to persevere and overcome the negative forces that work against us including our ego's resistance to change.

By mastering these assignments, I would eventually come to experience what Dr. Kavi referred to as *Divine Consciousness*—that is, the unification of self with the Divine Source. It is in this state of existence that you are able to transcend your humanness and accomplish your greatest deeds. *Divine Consciousness* explains how mortals like Michelangelo could sculpt The Pietà or paint the Sistine Chapel. *Divine Consciousness* explains how Leonardo da Vinci painted the Mona Lisa and fostered uncounted inventions hundreds of years before their time. *Divine Consciousness* also explains how Jesus could transcend his humanness and perform such extraordinary feats which we call miracles. As *The Course* teaches us, anything is possible when we use our divine powers!

CHAPTER 31

The Baltimore Conversation

In December, I traveled to Baltimore to meet Dr. Kavi and attend his lecture at Johns Hopkins University on *The Course of 10,000 Days®*. During his remarks, Dr. Kavi quoted Albert Einstein who said, "All conditions and all circumstances in our lives are a result of a certain level of thinking. If we want to change our conditions and circumstances, we have to change the level of thinking that is responsible."

Dr. Kavi spoke eloquently about the power of love and the detrimental effects on people who lack love or find it difficult to give love. He told the audience, "We are given life in order to experience and share the powers of love. Our higher purpose as human beings is to love ourselves and to love others. Love is our greatest gift and it is something that every human being is capable of giving and receiving."

Dr. Kavi also reminded the audience that we are all teachers and have an obligation to our communities and the world to teach others so that they might follow in our footsteps. Speaking the words of Henry Brooks Adams, Kavi told them, "A teacher affects eternity because he can never tell where his influence stops."

Later that evening, as we dined at Sotto Sopra's, Dr. Kavi reminded us that every life should be an expression of love, joy and meaning. This is why *The Course of 10,000 Days®* was created. And this is why the red rose was selected as the symbol for *The Course*. The color red represents energy, strength, passion, courage, career goals, fast action, desire, vibrancy, risk, love, determination, emotional intensity, leadership, excitement, warmth, generosity and romance. Our life should be a composite of all these things because we have been placed on earth to experience love in all its dimensions.

Remember, to experience love—to live a life worth remembering and attain our higher purpose—we must create a balance between our ego and our Inner Spirit. It is through this delicate dance that we learn to give as well as receive, to love others as well as ourselves, to accept those things we enjoy as well as those things we dislike, to work but also play and to grow in kindness, respect and love for ourselves and others. Dr. Kavi told me that love is a skill. Meaningful love is learned and practiced. It requires us to "train the mind and the senses so that our passions can be guided and transformed" as the spiritual guru Eknath Easwaran espouses.

Anyone who seeks to live *The Course* must be willing to make a fresh start. In the process of beginning anew, we must change our old habits. We must let go of our invalid and uncontested beliefs. We must end our grudges. We must also end the anger and resentment we harbor towards people and the hatred we hold in our hearts for those who have deeply hurt us. All these things must end. You cannot live *The Course* and hold onto negativity regardless of how it is disguised in your emotions, attitudes, beliefs and values. It does not work.

Dr. Kavi noted, "Times change, but certain guiding principles will always remain the same. Among the 12 guiding principles *The Course* teaches are:

1. An understanding and acceptance of yourself
2. A trusting relationship with your Inner Spirit
3. Respect for all living things
4. The ability to forgive instead of harboring anger, resentment and revenge
5. A thirst for knowledge
6. Pursuit of the truth
7. Embracing a healthy lifestyle that promotes wellness and extends your physical life while developing your mental faculties
8. Loyalty
9. Acting with courage
10. Generosity
11. Service to others
12. and, above all others, Love

CHAPTER 32

Living Your Next
10,000 Days

When students enroll in *The Course* weekend retreats, I can see in their eyes a sense of excitement as well as nervous anticipation. It's like riding a roller coaster. You're filled with anticipation but fearful of that first jolt and free-fall drop!

While there are no strenuous exercises or theatrics during *The Course* retreat, there is a definite sense of exhilaration and a rush of adrenaline attendees feel as they discover their higher purpose and how to tap into their Inner Spirit. Although the rush is more subdued than a roller coaster ride, the emotional highs are just as rewarding for an adult who is seeking love and trying to find fulfillment in his or her life.

There are four steps you can take today to begin the journey and create a life worth remembering:

1. Make the solemn commitment that you will live a purposeful life by creating a Personal Mission Statement in 20 words or less. For example, my personal mission statement is *to inspire, teach and nurture people in the ways of service, leadership and love.*

2. Define how you will *achieve* your personal mission. Describe exactly what you will do each day to live your personal mission. The Roman philosopher, Seneca, said that we should "Begin at once to live, and count each separate day as a separate life." In that spirit, create a Defining Statement which is different from your Mission Statement because it describes *how* you will achieve your Mission. For example, my Defining Statement is *I work with people and organizations that want to improve their lives and discover their higher purpose by guiding them through The Course of 10,000 Days®*.

3. Make a brief list (no more than 10 items) of the things you should do to initiate action and help you achieve your Mission. For example, your list might include the BAG It and BAGEL drill or taking a 20-minute daily walk to exercise your body and organize your thoughts. Or you might need to complete your application for a continuing education class or enroll in a personal development course. Be sure that each item you list is closely aligned to your Personal Mission Statement.

4. Get out of your own way. The biggest hurdle people must leap is the space between their ears! Eliminate the negative self-talk and replace it with written affirmations and positive thoughts that reinforce your goals instead of the reasons you cannot achieve them. Remember the 4:1 exercise Ajay gave me in our first conversation? Put it to work for you! Accentuate the positive instead of the negative.

Don't let the "old you" be the reason the "new you" doesn't succeed. Take it up a notch and persevere. Let the words of Ralph Marston's prose, *Take It Up a Notch*, inspire you.

It takes just as much effort to live poorly as it does to live well.
It takes just as much effort to be mediocre as it does to be magnificent.
As long as you're going to put in the time, you might as well make it count.

There are many people who pay to play golf, and there are some who get
paid millions of dollars to play golf. There are some people who earn a
few dollars per hour cooking food, and others who earn millions doing
it.
The difference is not the time or effort expended, but rather their
commitment to excellence.
The minimum wage cook is thinking about what he'll do when his shift
is over. The millionaire chef is thinking of ways to improve her food.
And they both get exactly what they dwell upon.
Whatever can be done, can be done better.
Your situation doesn't limit you.
There is opportunity for excellence in every situation.
Any limitations you have are the result of your own attitude.
Take it up a notch.
Aim a little higher today, and higher, yet tomorrow.
Think big.
Make it count, and make a difference.

While there are many people I admire, there are two men you should always think of whenever you begin to have doubts about your ability to succeed. The first is Francis Bernardone. He was a would-be troubadour and the son of an Italian cloth merchant. Francis squandered his youth by wandering from job to job and engaging in street brawls. During his imprisonment in Perugia he experienced a conversion and decided to devote his life to Jesus. We know him today as St. Francis of Assisi, one of the most beloved saints of the Catholic Church. His Prayer for Peace (see below) is among the most recited prayers in the world by people of all faiths and religions.

Lord, make me an instrument of your peace,
Where there is hatred, let me sow love;
where there is injury, pardon;
where there is doubt, faith;

where there is despair, hope;
where there is darkness, light;
where there is sadness, joy;
O Divine Master, grant that I may not
so much seek to be consoled as to console;
to be understood as to understand;
to be loved as to love.
For it is in giving that we receive;
it is in pardoning that we are pardoned;
and it is in dying that we are born to eternal life.

The second person was a talented attorney who earned his law degree in England and practiced law in India. After relocating to Pretoria, he grew tired of the discrimination and physical threats he experienced in South Africa, so he decided to dedicate his life to helping his fellow Indians win human rights from the British government. At the age of 45, he returned India to lead his native country's independence movement. We know him today as Mahatma Gandhi, one of the most admired human beings of the 20th century. While St. Francis and Gandhi gave us many lessons to live by, one of the most powerful lessons they taught us is to never underestimate the power of your convictions, the strength of your voice nor your commitment to the ideals you firmly believe. Just like Gandhi, others will rally to your cause if it is just.

My challenge to you is the same one that Dr. Kavi Chavan gave to me on that blistery December night in Baltimore. As we walked two blocks to our hotel in the freezing cold, Kavi told me, "In your lifetime, you will be tested many times in many different ways. But ultimately, your success will be determined by three things: (1) belief in yourself; (2) tried and tested values; and (3) your unbending resolve to live your higher purpose through your actions. So clearly define your dreams and goals. Have a plan for success. And do something every day, whether it is a simple act of kindness or a significant achievement that brings you closer to fulfilling your dreams. There is no one else who can do it for you. It is completely up to you."

During dinner, Kavi referenced the words of mythologist Joseph Campbell, who believed we must follow our bliss. Campbell reminds us that when we follow our bliss we begin to meet the right people who will open doors that will lead us to a better place. I knew my bliss would be found in teaching *The Course*.

When I first met Ajay many years ago, I didn't know how our relationship would evolve and change my life. I just trusted my instincts and allowed my Inner Spirit to guide me. Oftentimes, our ego and Inner Spirit work in serendipitous ways. My relationship with Ajay progressed from that of a client to a friend and spiritual counselor. Ultimately, it opened a door that led me to undertake *The Course of 10,000 Days®*, write this book and now teach *The Course*. During this journey, I have reconnected with my Inner Spirit and discovered my higher purpose. This discovery also led me to Dr. Kavi and many other wonderful people who have been my mentors and teachers.

As I look back on my journey and what I learned from *The Course*, I realize that everything I have ever asked for that was consistent with my higher purpose has been granted to me. I cannot think of any significant exceptions! I am not talking about ego-driven requests like winning the lottery, but rather those things that are necessary in one's life to create balance, harmony and happiness. I am talking about those intrinsic assets like wisdom, grace, love, purpose, peace and a passion for living.

Now, I am living my higher purpose and helping others follow their bliss. I have come full circle because *The Course* has led me to you. I invite you to begin a new chapter in your life as you emerge from your Fulfillment Years and begin your Legacy Years. Follow your bliss and embrace *The Course of 10,000 Days®*.

CHAPTER 33

About
The Course of 10,000 Days®
Weekend Retreat

Are you interested in applying what you've learned in 10,000 Days to improve your life and achieve your goals and dreams? If so, The 10,000 Days Foundation invites you to join us for *The Course of 10,000 Days®* Weekend Retreat featuring author Tom Hinton and a talented faculty of practitioners, coaches and trainers.

During this three-day event, you'll discover the secret to finding your higher purpose, how to attain inner peace and renew your passion for those things that are significant in your life. You'll also learn how to apply the eight elements from The 10,000 Days Wheel of Life (see page 256) in your everyday life.

Join thought leader Tom Hinton and other experts as they guide you on a remarkable, experiential journey to help you focus on your goals and dreams, create a 100-Day Life Action Plan for Success and lead you to your higher purpose! You will also learn how to balance and control your Ego while allowing your Inner Spirit to surface and soar!

Among the questions and issues you'll explore during *The Course* Weekend Retreat are these 12 guiding principles:

1. An understanding and acceptance of yourself
2. A trusting relationship with your Inner Spirit
3. Respect for all living things
4. The ability to forgive instead of harboring anger, resentment and revenge
5. A thirst for knowledge
6. Pursuit of the truth
7. Embracing a healthy lifestyle that promotes wellness and extends your physical life while developing your mental faculties
8. Loyalty
9. Acting with courage
10. Generosity
11. Service to others
12. and, above all others, Love

Visit www.10000Days.org today to obtain our most current schedule of events or to enroll in *The Course of 10,000 Days*®. We look forward to welcoming you to the first day of the "best of your life!"

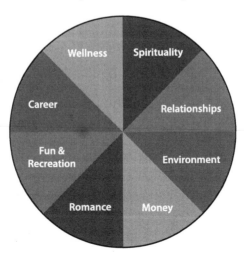

Addendum

The Seven Natural Laws are:

1. *The Law of Perpetual Transmutation.* This law states that energy moves into a physical form. And the images you hold in your mind most often materialize in your life. *The Course* suggests we picture positive images and focus on those things we desire as opposed to thinking about the things we don't want to happen. Accentuate the positive!

2. *The Law of Relativity.* This law states that nothing is good or bad, big or small, etc. until you relate it to something. *The Course* suggests we compare our current problems or negative situation to something much worse, and we will find our situation doesn't look as bad as the other fellow's problem.

3. *The Law of Vibration and Attraction.* This law states that everything in the universe vibrates. Nothing rests. One's conscious awareness of vibration is called *feeling.* Our thoughts control our ideas and vibrations. This, in turn, dictates what we attract. *The Course* suggests when you are not feeling good or not thinking positive thoughts it helps to become aware of what you're thinking and change your thoughts from negative to positive. This will change your vibrations and allow you to attract better outcomes in your life.

4. *The Law of Polarity.* This law states that everything has an opposite. As I discussed in *10,000 Days,* there is hot and cold, fire and rain, good and evil, up and down and so forth. *The Course* suggests we look for the good in people and situations. When you find it, share positive thoughts with people because we all like to be

complimented. It makes us feel good. Also, remember that positive thoughts send out positive vibrations and attract good things into our life. It should be noted obviously that disastrous events and tragedies occur in life; and frankly, it's very difficult to see any good resulting from such events. Nevertheless, in such difficult times, our prayers and positive energy can be a comfort to those who are suffering. Perhaps then, this is the good that results from such occurrences.

5. **The Law of Rhythm.** This law states that all things in the universe follow a natural process or rhythm. Just as sunrise is followed by sunset, night follows day. *The Course* suggests when we are on the receiving end of bad news or hard times, it is important to recognize that eventually things will shift and get better. Good times are coming. However, it is your thoughts and actions that will dictate the timing of better outcomes.

6. **The Law of Cause and Effect.** This law states that whatever you send into the universe it comes back to you. For every action there is a reaction. *The Course* suggests we be aware of our thoughts and actions and direct positive energy outward so that our life is enriched and blessed with good things and positive results. Also, don't worry about what you're going to receive. Rather, focus on what you can give to others.

7. **The Law of Gender.** This law states that every seed has an incubation or gestation period. Our ideas, aspirations and hopes are actually spiritual seeds that will take form and generate physical results if we simply tend to them as a gardener cares for his roses. *The Course* suggests we focus our energies on those things we desire. In this way, our hopes and dreams will take root and eventually become reality.

[1] See the Addendum for more information on the 7 Natural Laws of the Universe.

The Course
Invites Your Feedback:

As you read *10,000 Days* and complete the various exercises associated with *The Course of 10,000 Days*®, we would like to hear from you. It would be very helpful to know what helped you on your journey to find purpose, peace and abundance in your life. One of our goals at the 10,000 Days Foundation is to build an international community of practitioners who can share their experiences, successes, shortcomings, frustrations, questions and revelations about *The Course of 10,000 Days*®. Please visit our website and let us know your thoughts. You can comment at: http://www.10000days.org/contact.asp

We are also looking for new ideas, exercises and methods to make *The Course of 10,000 Days*® more meaningful and relevant for our attendees and participants. By sharing your experiences, we can improve future weekend retreats, mini-workshops, online programs and webinars. Any information you share with us will be treated confidentially. If you have questions, please let us know and a staff member of the 10,000 Days Foundation will follow-up with you by email. So be sure to include your email address.

Thanks for helping us make *The Course of 10,000 Days*® a meaningful experience for everyone!

About the Author

Since 1989, Tom Hinton has inspired, challenged, nurtured and entertained nearly 1,000 corporate, association, and government audiences with his dynamic speeches and interactive workshops on personal growth and professional development topics including: Work-Life Balance, How to Make the Rest of Your Life the Best of Your Life and Creating a Culture of Excellence in the Workplace.

In 2006, Tom completed *The Course of 10,000 Days*®, a transformational personal development program that dramatically altered his perspective on how to live a life of purpose, peace and happiness. Today, Tom teaches audiences how to create the life of their dreams and make the rest of your life the best of your life through the principles and practices embodied in *The Course of 10,000 Days*®. He continues to speak around the world to corporate audiences and facilitate public workshops on these timely issues and popular topics.

Tom also serves as the chairman of The 10,000 Days Foundation, a non-profit personal growth organization based in San Diego, California that is dedicated to helping people find their higher purpose through *The Course of 10,000 Days*® and creating spiritual balance, fulfillment and prosperity in their lives.

Tom is a graduate of the University of Maryland and the author of five books. He can be reached via email at: tom@10000Days.org or via the website: www.10000Days.org

Index